Paws, Claws, and Fins

A Captivating Guide to Animal Adaptations and Survival

Shae Gill

The presentation of the information is without contract or any type of guarantee assurance. The trademarks that are used are without any consent, and the publication of the trademark is without permission or backing by the trademark owner. All trademarks and brands within this book are for clarifying purposes only and are the owned by the owners themselves, not affiliated with this document.

Table of Contents

Chapter 1

Introduction to Animal Adaptations

The Importance of Adaptations

Adaptations are the lifeblood of the natural world, the very essence of how life thrives amidst the ever-changing tapestry of Earth's environments. They serve as the bridge between the raw, pulsating vigor of life and the relentless forces of nature, ensuring that species not only survive but thrive in diverse habitats. At its core, adaptation is the process by which organisms adjust and refine their physical structures, behaviors, and physiological processes in response to the demands and challenges posed by their surroundings. This dynamic interplay between biology and environment has given rise to the breathtaking diversity of life we see today.

In the grand theater of evolution, each species is both actor and audience, engaged in an ongoing performance where the script is never set in stone. Adaptations emerge over countless generations, sculpted by the invisible hand of natural selection. This process, first articulated by Charles Darwin, is the mechanism by which the fittest individuals—those best suited to their environments—pass on their genetic material to future generations. Over time, these incremental changes accumulate, leading to the emergence of traits that enhance survival and reproductive success.

Consider the polar bear, an emblematic figure of adaptation to extreme cold. With its thick layer of blubber, dense fur, and white coat that camouflages against the snow, the polar bear is a master of arctic survival. This majestic creature exemplifies how species evolve physical characteristics tailored to their environment. Similarly, the chameleon, with its remarkable ability to change skin color, illustrates how adaptive traits can aid in both camouflage and communication, playing crucial roles in avoiding predators and finding mates.

Behavioral adaptations, too, are a vital component of survival strategies. These are not etched in the physical form but are learned and passed on through generations. The migratory patterns of birds, honed over millennia, are a testament to this. Each year, millions of avian travelers embark on epic journeys across continents, instinctively navigating vast distances to exploit seasonal resources. The precision of these migrations—guided by an innate understanding of geography and climate—demonstrates the profound influence of behavioral adaptations on survival.

Adaptations also extend to the intricate symbiotic relationships that define ecosystems. The mutualistic bond between bees and flowering plants is a classic example. Bees, in their quest for nectar, inadvertently transfer pollen from one flower to another, facilitating reproduction. This exchange benefits both parties, highlighting how adaptations can foster interdependence and cooperation among species. Such relationships underscore the complexity of ecosystems, where survival often hinges not on solitary efforts but on collaboration and mutual benefit.

The environment is an ever-shifting mosaic of challenges and opportunities, and species must remain agile in their adaptations to persist. Climate change, habitat destruction, and pollution are contemporary threats that test the adaptive capabilities of species worldwide. Some, like the urban-dwelling pigeon, have thrived in human-altered landscapes, showcasing remarkable plasticity in behavior and diet. Others, however, such as the critically endangered Sumatran orangutan, face dire threats as their habitats vanish. These contrasting fates illustrate the critical importance of adaptability in the face of rapid environmental changes.

Adaptations are not confined to the present; they are a historical narrative written in the DNA of all living organisms. The fossil record is a testament to the myriad forms life has taken, each a chapter in the story of adaptation. From the armored scales of ancient fish to the feathers of early avian ancestors, these relics offer glimpses into the evolutionary past, revealing how species have continually reinvented themselves in response to shifting landscapes and climates.

The importance of adaptations extends beyond individual species; it shapes entire ecosystems and influences biodiversity. A diverse range of adaptations contributes to the stability and resilience of ecosystems, allowing them to withstand disturbances and maintain ecological balance. In a rainforest, for example, the myriad adaptations of plants, insects, birds, and mammals create a complex web of interactions that sustains the entire community. The loss of even a single species can ripple through this web, underscoring the interconnectedness of life and the critical role adaptations play in maintaining ecological harmony.

In understanding the importance of adaptations, one must also acknowledge their limitations. Not all species can adapt quickly enough to survive sudden or drastic changes. The extinction of the dodo, a flightless bird native to Mauritius, serves as a poignant reminder of this. The dodo's inability to adapt to the arrival of humans and introduced species led to its rapid demise, highlighting the fragile balance between adaptation and extinction.

Adaptations are a testament to the ingenuity and resilience of life on Earth. They are the result of countless generations of trial and error, a testament to the relentless drive of species to persist and flourish. In studying adaptations, we gain a deeper appreciation for the complexity of life and the intricate dance between organisms and their environments. This understanding is not merely academic; it has practical implications for conservation efforts, guiding strategies to protect endangered species and preserve the delicate balance of ecosystems.

Evolutionary Roots of Adaptation

Delving into the evolutionary roots of adaptation unveils a captivating narrative of life's persistent quest for survival. Every organism on Earth is a testament to millions of years of evolutionary fine-tuning, an ongoing saga that began with the earliest forms of life and continues to this day. The story of adaptation is one of resilience, innovation, and transformation, as species navigate the myriad challenges posed by their environments.

The concept of adaptation is deeply intertwined with the theory of evolution, first brought to prominence by Charles Darwin. His groundbreaking work, "On the Origin of Species," introduced the world to natural selection, a mechanism by which advantageous traits become more common in a population over successive generations. This selective process is the driving force behind adaptation, shaping species to better fit their ecological niches. Through natural selection, those individuals with traits that enhance survival and reproduction are more likely to pass on their genes, gradually leading to populations that are finely tuned to their environments.

The evolutionary journey of adaptation begins at the molecular level, where genetic mutations provide the raw material for evolutionary change. Mutations, while often neutral or even detrimental, occasionally produce variations that confer an advantage in a specific context. These beneficial mutations can alter an organism's physiology, morphology, or behavior, setting the stage for adaptation. Over time, as these advantageous traits accumulate, they form the foundation of the complex adaptations observed in the natural world.

Consider the evolution of the giraffe's elongated neck, a quintessential example of adaptation through natural selection. Ancestors of modern giraffes once roamed the African savannas, competing for resources in a landscape dominated by tall trees. Individuals with slightly longer necks could reach higher foliage, accessing a food source unavailable to their shorter-necked peers. This seemingly small advantage, when compounded over countless generations, led to the remarkable neck length seen in giraffes today. Such adaptations highlight the power of natural selection in shaping traits that confer survival advantages.

Adaptations can also arise from a process known as genetic drift, which involves random changes in gene frequency within a population. Unlike natural selection, genetic drift does not necessarily favor advantageous traits; instead, it introduces variability that can lead to new adaptations under changing environmental conditions. This randomness can be particularly influential in small populations, where chance events can have a significant impact on genetic diversity. Genetic drift, alongside natural selection, contributes to the rich tapestry of adaptations that characterize life on Earth.

The evolutionary roots of adaptation are further influenced by the phenomenon of coevolution, where species evolve in response to one another, creating a dynamic interplay of adaptations. Predator-prey relationships exemplify this intricate dance, as each party develops strategies to outwit the other. In the African savanna, the cheetah's explosive speed has evolved in tandem with the gazelle's agility and evasive maneuvers, resulting in a continuous arms race of adaptations. Such coevolutionary dynamics illustrate the interconnectedness of life, where the adaptation of one species can drive evolutionary changes in another.

Adaptations are not solely the domain of individual species; they also shape entire ecosystems. Ecosystem-level adaptations emerge from the collective interactions of organisms within a community, influencing processes such as nutrient cycling, energy flow, and ecological balance. In coral reefs, for instance, the myriad adaptations of corals, fish, and invertebrates create a vibrant and resilient ecosystem capable of withstanding environmental fluctuations. These adaptations enhance the stability and productivity of the reef, underscoring the pivotal role of adaptation in ecosystem dynamics.

The fossil record provides a window into the evolutionary history of adaptations, offering insights into the forms life has taken over geological time. Fossils reveal the gradual emergence of adaptations in response to environmental pressures, painting a picture of life's evolutionary journey. The transition from aquatic to terrestrial life, as evidenced by the fossilized remains of early tetrapods, showcases the profound impact of adaptation on the diversification of life. These ancient pioneers evolved limbs capable of supporting their weight on land, a pivotal adaptation that paved the way for the proliferation of terrestrial vertebrates.

Adaptations also reflect the constraints and trade-offs inherent in evolutionary processes. While adaptations enhance an organism's fitness in a particular context, they may also impose limitations. The panda's specialized diet of bamboo, for example, represents a trade-off between dietary specialization and nutritional flexibility. Such constraints highlight the complex interplay between adaptation and the environment, where the benefits of a particular trait must be balanced against its potential drawbacks.

The study of adaptations offers profound insights into the resilience and creativity of life. As environments continue to change, species must adapt or face extinction, a reality that underscores the urgency of understanding the mechanisms underlying adaptation. Climate change, habitat destruction, and other anthropogenic threats pose unprecedented challenges to species worldwide, testing their adaptive capacities. Conservation efforts, informed by evolutionary principles, seek to preserve the genetic diversity and adaptive potential of species, ensuring their survival in an uncertain future.

Types of Adaptations Physical and Behavioral

Adaptations, the remarkable adjustments organisms make to thrive in their environments, can be broadly classified into physical and behavioral types. These adaptations shape the way species interact with their surroundings and each other, influencing their chances of survival and reproduction. Understanding the nuances of physical and behavioral adaptations offers insight into the diversity of life and the strategies employed by different species to navigate the challenges of existence.

Physical adaptations refer to the structural and physiological changes that enhance an organism's ability to survive in its habitat. These modifications often manifest in the form of body structures, coloration, and internal processes that improve an organism's ability to find food, avoid predators, and withstand environmental conditions. Take the example of the Arctic fox, whose thick fur, compact body shape, and seasonal color change are quintessential physical adaptations. The dense fur provides insulation against frigid temperatures, while the compact body minimizes heat loss. In winter, the fox's coat turns white, offering camouflage against the snowy landscape, a crucial adaptation for both predation and avoiding predators.

Another example of physical adaptation is the impressive beak diversity found among Darwin's finches in the Galápagos Islands. These birds have evolved a variety of beak shapes and sizes, each suited to a specific dietary niche. Finches with robust, large beaks can crack open hard seeds, while those with slender, pointed beaks excel at extracting insects from crevices. Such diversity not only illustrates how physical adaptations can enable species to exploit different food sources but also highlights the role of adaptation in reducing competition and promoting coexistence.

Physical adaptations extend beyond external structures to include physiological processes that equip organisms to thrive in specific environments. The camel, with its ability to endure long periods without water, exemplifies such adaptations. Its kidneys conserve water efficiently, and its blood cells can swell to hold more water without rupturing. These physiological traits allow camels to traverse arid deserts, where water is scarce. Similarly, the kangaroo rat, native to North American deserts, has evolved kidneys that excrete minimal water, enabling it to survive on a diet of dry seeds.

In contrast to physical adaptations, behavioral adaptations involve changes in an organism's actions that enhance survival and reproductive success. These adaptations often develop in response to environmental stimuli and can be learned or instinctual. Migration is a prime example of a behavioral adaptation, seen in countless species from birds to butterflies. Monarch butterflies, for instance, embark on an astounding migration spanning thousands of miles from North America to central Mexico. This behavior allows them to escape harsh winter conditions and find suitable breeding grounds, ensuring the survival of the species.

Another fascinating behavioral adaptation is hibernation, employed by many animals to cope with seasonal resource scarcity. Bears, for instance, enter a state of dormancy during the winter months, reducing their metabolic rate and conserving energy when food is scarce. This adaptation not only helps them survive the winter but also allows them to emerge in spring ready to take advantage of the newfound abundance of food.

Some species exhibit complex social behaviors as adaptive strategies. Wolves, for example, hunt in packs, a behavior that enhances their ability to capture large prey and defend territory. This cooperative hunting strategy is a testament to how social behavior can improve survival and reproductive success. Similarly, eusocial insects like ants and bees showcase intricate social structures where individuals perform specific roles for the benefit of the colony.

The division of labor and cooperative brood care in these colonies exemplify how behavioral adaptations can lead to highly efficient and successful communities.

Behavioral adaptations also include communication strategies, which are vital for mating, foraging, and avoiding predators. Many bird species utilize elaborate songs and visual displays to attract mates and establish territory. These behaviors are adaptations that enhance reproductive success by ensuring that individuals select mates with the best genes and establish dominance in resource-rich areas. In the marine world, dolphins use sophisticated vocalizations and echolocation to communicate and hunt, demonstrating how behavior can be an essential tool for survival.

The interplay between physical and behavioral adaptations often results in a synergy that enhances an organism's overall fitness. The cheetah, the fastest land animal, exhibits both types of adaptations. Its slender, aerodynamic body and powerful leg muscles are physical traits that enable incredible speed. However, its hunting strategy, which involves stalking prey to get as close as possible before launching a high-speed chase, is a behavioral adaptation that increases the likelihood of a successful hunt. Together, these adaptations make the cheetah a formidable predator on the African savanna.

Adaptations are not static; they evolve over time as environments change. The flexibility of behavioral adaptations allows species to respond more rapidly to short-term changes, while physical adaptations often reflect long-term evolutionary pressures. This dynamic nature of adaptation underscores the resilience and ingenuity of life on Earth, as species continually adjust to the shifting ecological landscape.

Survival of the Fittest Natural Selection in Action

The concept of "survival of the fittest," a phrase often synonymous with Charles Darwin's theory of natural selection, captures the essence of the relentless struggle for existence that shapes the natural world. This principle describes the process by which individuals with advantageous traits are more likely to survive, reproduce, and pass on their genetic material to the next generation. Over time, this leads to the proliferation of those traits within a population, tailoring species to their environments and driving the evolutionary process.

Natural selection acts on the variation that exists within a population. This variation arises from genetic mutations, sexual reproduction, and genetic recombination, all of which introduce new traits or modify existing ones. These traits can influence an organism's ability to secure resources, avoid predators, and adapt to environmental changes. The environment, with its myriad challenges and opportunities, serves as the arena in which natural selection operates, determining which individuals are most fit to thrive.

The Galápagos Islands, a remote archipelago in the Pacific Ocean, provide a living laboratory for observing natural selection in action. Among its most famous inhabitants are Darwin's finches, a group of bird species that have evolved a wide range of beak shapes and sizes. These adaptations are a direct response to the diverse food sources available on the islands. During periods of drought, when seeds become scarce, finches with beak shapes best suited to accessing available food are more likely to survive and reproduce. This dynamic interplay between environmental conditions and beak morphology illustrates the power of natural selection to drive adaptation and diversification.

Natural selection is not limited to physical traits; it also shapes behaviors that enhance survival and reproductive success. The hunting strategies of predators, the evasive maneuvers of prey, and the complex social structures of certain species have all been refined through this process. Consider the social hierarchy of lion prides, where cooperation among females during hunting increases the likelihood of a successful kill. This cooperative behavior, honed by natural selection, ensures the survival of the pride's members and the continuation of their genetic lineage.

The process of natural selection is not always gradual. In some instances, rapid environmental changes can lead to swift evolutionary responses. This phenomenon, known as "punctuated equilibrium," suggests that species remain relatively stable for long periods until a sudden shift in the environment demands rapid adaptation. The peppered moth in England provides a classic example of this. During the Industrial Revolution, soot from factories darkened the bark of trees, making the once-common light-colored moths more visible to predators. In response, the frequency of darker-colored moths increased dramatically, illustrating the speed at which natural selection can operate when conditions change abruptly.

While natural selection is a powerful force in shaping species, it is important to recognize that it operates within the constraints of existing genetic variation. Not all traits that arise are beneficial, and some may even be detrimental. Additionally, natural selection can only act on traits that are heritable, meaning they can be passed from one generation to the next. This limitation underscores the importance of genetic diversity within populations, as it provides the raw material for evolution and adaptation.

The interplay between natural selection and genetic drift, another evolutionary mechanism, further complicates the picture. Genetic drift, unlike natural selection, is a random process that can lead to changes in trait frequencies within a population. This randomness can be particularly pronounced in small populations, where chance events can have a significant impact on genetic diversity. While genetic drift can introduce new variations, it can also lead to the loss of beneficial traits, highlighting the intricate balance between stability and change in evolutionary dynamics.

The concept of "survival of the fittest" extends beyond individual species to encompass entire ecosystems. Natural selection shapes the interactions between species, influencing the balance of power between predators and prey, competitors, and cooperative partners. In a coral reef ecosystem, for example, the myriad adaptations of corals, fish, and invertebrates create a complex web of relationships that sustain the community. The success of one species often hinges on the adaptations of others, illustrating the interconnectedness of life and the role of natural selection in maintaining ecological balance.

The application of natural selection extends to human endeavors, where understanding evolutionary principles can inform conservation efforts and medical research. Conservationists use insights from natural selection to develop strategies for preserving endangered species, focusing on maintaining genetic diversity and adaptive potential. In medicine, the study of antibiotic resistance in bacteria highlights the ongoing battle between natural selection and human intervention, as resistant strains evolve in response to the widespread use of antibiotics.

Despite its explanatory power, the concept of "survival of the fittest" is often misunderstood. It does not imply that only the strongest or most aggressive individuals survive; rather, fitness refers to an organism's ability to reproduce and pass on its genes. This can involve a wide range of strategies, from cooperation and altruism to specialization and innovation. The diverse array of life on Earth is a testament to the myriad ways in which natural selection can shape survival strategies, each uniquely suited to the challenges of a particular environment.

The Role of Environment in Shaping Adaptations

The environment plays a pivotal role in shaping the remarkable adaptations observed in the natural world. It acts as both sculptor and stage, crafting the traits and behaviors that allow organisms to thrive in diverse ecological niches. This dynamic relationship between environment and adaptation is driven by an array of factors, including climate, geography, resource availability, and ecological interactions.

At the heart of this relationship lies the concept of environmental pressures, which are the forces that push species to adapt in order to survive and reproduce. These pressures can be as subtle as a gradual change in temperature or as abrupt as a volcanic eruption. The ability of a species to respond to these pressures determines its success and longevity in a given habitat.

Climate is one of the most influential environmental factors in shaping adaptations. It dictates the temperature, humidity, and seasonality of an area, creating specific conditions to which organisms must adjust. In polar regions, where temperatures plummet to extreme lows, animals like the Arctic fox and penguin have evolved thick layers of insulation to conserve heat. Conversely, in the scorching deserts of the Sahara, creatures such as the fennec fox and camel have developed adaptations to dissipate heat and conserve water, allowing them to endure the relentless sun and scarce resources.

Geographical barriers such as mountains, rivers, and oceans further influence the development of adaptations by isolating populations and limiting gene flow. This isolation can lead to the emergence of unique traits as populations adapt to their distinct environments. The diverse finch species of the Galápagos Islands, each with its own specialized beak shape, are a classic example of how geographic isolation can drive adaptive radiation. These birds have evolved to exploit different food sources, reducing competition and allowing multiple species to coexist.

Resource availability is another critical factor that shapes adaptations. The presence or absence of food, water, shelter, and mates can drive the development of traits that enhance an organism's ability to secure these resources. In nutrient-poor environments, such as the acidic waters of bogs and swamps, carnivorous plants like the Venus flytrap have adopted unique feeding strategies to supplement their nutritional intake. By capturing and digesting insects, they obtain essential nutrients that are scarce in their environment, demonstrating how adaptations can arise from resource scarcity.

Ecological interactions, including competition, predation, and mutualism, also play a significant role in shaping adaptations. These interactions create a complex web of relationships that influence the evolutionary trajectory of species. Predation pressure, for instance, has led to the development of a stunning array of defensive adaptations, from the cryptic coloration of the stick insect to the venomous spines of the lionfish. These traits enhance an organism's ability to avoid detection or deter predators, increasing its chances of survival.

Mutualistic relationships, where two or more species benefit from each other's presence, can also drive the evolution of adaptations. The relationship between bees and flowering plants is a quintessential example. Flowers have evolved vibrant colors, alluring scents, and nectar rewards to attract pollinators, while bees have developed specialized body parts to collect and transfer pollen. This mutualism not only highlights the role of ecological interactions in shaping adaptations but also underscores the interconnectedness of life. activity has become an increasingly significant environmental factor influencing adaptations. Urbanization, pollution, and climate change are reshaping habitats and exerting new pressures on species. Some organisms, like the urban pigeon, have shown remarkable adaptability to human-altered environments, developing new behaviors and dietary preferences. Others, however, struggle to cope with rapid changes, leading to population declines and extinctions.

The impact of human activity on the environment also extends to the introduction of invasive species, which can disrupt established ecosystems and create novel selection pressures. The introduction of the brown tree snake to Guam, for example, has led to the decline of native bird populations, illustrating how invasive species can drive adaptive responses in native organisms or lead to their eradication.

Adaptations are evidence of life's resilience in the face of environmental challenges. They are the product of countless generations of interaction between organisms and their environments, reflecting a delicate balance between stability and change. As environments continue to evolve, species must remain flexible and responsive to survive. This ongoing dance between adaptation and environment is a testament to the dynamic nature of life on Earth.

Understanding the role of environment in shaping adaptations provides valuable insights into the mechanisms of evolution and the resilience of ecosystems. It highlights the importance of preserving diverse habitats and ecological processes, ensuring that species have the opportunity to adapt to changing conditions. As stewards of the planet, humans have a responsibility to mitigate the impact of our activities on the environment, safeguarding the remarkable diversity of life and its capacity to adapt.

Chapter 2

Land Dwellers Mastering the Terrain

The Majesty of Mammals Adaptations for Land Living

Mammals, with their diverse forms and fascinating adaptations, have successfully colonized nearly every terrestrial habitat on Earth. Their evolutionary journey from aquatic ancestors to dominant land-dwelling creatures showcases a wealth of adaptations that have enabled them to thrive in varied environments. These adaptations, both structural and behavioral, underscore the majesty of mammals and their ability to navigate the challenges of terrestrial life.

One of the most significant adaptations that facilitated the transition from water to land is the development of a robust skeletal system. The transition to a land-based existence required mammals to support their body weight against gravity. Over millions of years, their skeletons evolved to provide the necessary support and mobility. The vertebral column, for instance, became more flexible and capable of supporting diverse forms of locomotion, from the bounding leaps of a kangaroo to the stealthy prowl of a jaguar. Limbs evolved into various configurations, each suited to the specific needs of different species, whether it be the slender legs of a gazelle for swift running or the powerful limbs of an elephant for bearing immense weight.

Mammals also developed advanced respiratory and circulatory systems to meet the demands of land living. The evolution of a diaphragm, a muscular partition that aids in breathing, allowed for more efficient oxygen intake. This adaptation is crucial for sustaining high levels of activity and energy expenditure, which are often required in terrestrial habitats. The circulatory system, too, became more efficient, with a four-chambered heart that ensures the separation of oxygenated and deoxygenated blood, allowing for a steady supply of oxygen to muscles during vigorous activities.

The evolution of endothermy, or warm-bloodedness, represents another key adaptation. Endothermy allows mammals to maintain a stable internal body temperature regardless of external conditions, granting them the ability to inhabit a wide range of environments. This adaptation is supported by fur or hair, which provides insulation and helps regulate body temperature. In colder climates, mammals like polar bears and arctic foxes have developed thick, insulating fur to conserve heat, while desert dwellers like camels have sparse coats to dissipate heat and avoid overheating.

Mammalian sensory adaptations are equally remarkable, enabling them to interact with and respond to their environments effectively. Many mammals have developed keen senses of smell and hearing, which are essential for detecting predators, locating prey, and navigating their surroundings. The olfactory system in canines, for example, is highly developed, allowing them to track scents over vast distances. Bats, on the other hand, have evolved echolocation, a sophisticated system of navigation and prey detection that relies on sound waves. These sensory adaptations highlight the diverse strategies mammals employ to survive and thrive in different habitats.

Reproductive adaptations also play a crucial role in the success of mammals on land. The development of internal fertilization and live birth in most species offers several advantages, including protection of the young during development and the ability to give birth in various environments. Parental care, a hallmark of mammalian reproduction, ensures that offspring receive the necessary nourishment and protection during their early stages of life. This investment in young significantly enhances their chances of survival, allowing mammal populations to flourish.

Behavioral adaptations further illustrate the majesty of mammals, as they have evolved complex social structures and communication systems to enhance survival. Many mammals, such as elephants and primates, exhibit intricate social behaviors, forming tight-knit groups that provide protection, cooperation in hunting or foraging, and shared knowledge that aids in navigating their environments. Communication, both vocal and non-vocal, is vital in maintaining these social bonds and coordinating group activities. Dolphins, for example, use a complex array of clicks and whistles to convey information and coordinate group behavior, demonstrating the depth of mammalian communication.

The ability to adapt behaviorally to environmental changes is another testament to the resilience of mammals. Many species exhibit flexibility in their diet, foraging strategies, and habitat use, allowing them to respond to shifts in resource availability or environmental conditions. The raccoon, with its omnivorous diet and opportunistic foraging habits, exemplifies this adaptability. Its success in both rural and urban environments highlights the versatility of behavioral adaptations in mammals.

The diverse adaptations of mammals for land living are not only a testament to their evolutionary success but also a source of inspiration for understanding the interplay between organisms and their environments. As mammals continue to adapt to changing conditions, they offer valuable insights into the processes that drive evolution and the resilience of life on Earth. The challenges posed by habitat loss, climate change, and human activities underscore the importance of conserving mammalian diversity and the ecosystems they inhabit.

Reptilian Resilience Surviving in Diverse Climates

Reptiles, with their ancient lineage and remarkable adaptability, have mastered the art of survival across a vast array of climates. Their resilience is a testament to the evolutionary innovations that enable them to thrive in environments ranging from scorching deserts to humid rainforests. These adaptations highlight the intricate relationship between reptiles and their habitats, offering insight into the strategies that have allowed them to persist through the ages.

One of the most striking adaptations of reptiles is their ectothermic physiology, which allows them to regulate body temperature through external means rather than internal metabolic processes. This strategy minimizes energy expenditure, a crucial advantage in environments where resources may be scarce or conditions harsh. In deserts, where temperatures can fluctuate dramatically between day and night, reptiles like the Gila monster and the desert tortoise exhibit behavioral thermoregulation. By basking in the sun to absorb heat and retreating to shaded burrows to cool down, they maintain optimal body temperatures for survival.

Desert reptiles have also evolved physiological adaptations to conserve water, an essential resource in arid regions. Many possess highly efficient kidneys that excrete waste with minimal water loss. The thorny devil, an Australian lizard, showcases an extraordinary adaptation in its skin, which can channel moisture from rainfall or dew directly to its mouth. This unique method of water collection exemplifies the innovative strategies reptiles employ to endure the challenges of desert life.

In contrast to the arid desert dwellers, reptiles inhabiting tropical rainforests must navigate a world of intense humidity and dense vegetation. The green tree python, for example, exhibits arboreal adaptations that allow it to maneuver effortlessly through the forest canopy. Its prehensile tail aids in climbing, while its vibrant green coloration provides camouflage among the leaves, protecting it from predators and helping it ambush prey. Such adaptations illustrate the versatility of reptiles in exploiting the diverse resources of their environments.

The ability to survive in cold climates is another testament to reptilian resilience. Although traditionally associated with warmer regions, some reptiles have adapted to life in cooler areas. The common garter snake, found in North America, exhibits brumation—a state of dormancy similar to hibernation—during the winter months. By slowing their metabolism and seeking refuge in communal hibernacula, these snakes conserve energy and endure the cold until conditions improve. This behavior underscores the flexibility of reptiles in adjusting to seasonal changes.

Reptiles also display remarkable adaptability in their reproductive strategies, which contribute to their survival across diverse climates. Many species lay eggs with tough, leathery shells that offer protection from environmental extremes. Some, like the American alligator, construct nests that utilize decaying vegetation to generate heat, ensuring the proper incubation temperature for their eggs. This adaptation highlights the ingenuity of reptiles in safeguarding the next generation, even in challenging environments.

Parental care, though less common in reptiles than in mammals or birds, is another strategy that enhances survival. The king cobra, for instance, is known for its protective behavior toward its eggs, guarding the nest against potential threats until the young hatch. This investment in offspring, though rare in the reptilian world, demonstrates the evolutionary drive to ensure the continuation of the species.

In addition to physiological and behavioral adaptations, reptiles possess defensive mechanisms that enhance their resilience. Camouflage is a common strategy, with many species evolving coloration and patterns that blend seamlessly into their surroundings. The horned lizard, for example, not only uses cryptic coloration to avoid detection but also employs an unusual defense mechanism: it can squirt blood from its eyes to deter predators. Such adaptations illustrate the lengths to which reptiles will go to ensure their survival.

The resilience of reptiles is further demonstrated by their ability to exploit human-altered environments. Some species, like the common wall lizard, have thrived in urban settings, capitalizing on the warm microclimates created by concrete structures and the abundance of food sources. This adaptability to human presence highlights the capacity of reptiles to adjust to new challenges and opportunities, a trait that has contributed to their enduring success.

Despite their resilience, reptiles face numerous threats from habitat destruction, climate change, and human activities. Conservation efforts are crucial to preserving their diversity and ensuring their continued survival. Understanding the adaptations that have allowed reptiles to thrive can inform strategies to protect their habitats and mitigate the impact of environmental changes. By fostering coexistence between reptiles and humans, we can safeguard the future of these remarkable creatures.

Amphibious Wonders Dual Life Strategies

Amphibians, the remarkable creatures that bridge the gap between aquatic and terrestrial life, epitomize the concept of dual life strategies. Their evolutionary path reveals a fascinating blend of adaptations that enable them to thrive in both water and on land. These adaptations not only reflect their ancient lineage but also highlight their ability to navigate the challenges posed by fluctuating environments.

The hallmark of amphibians is their life cycle, which typically begins in water and transitions to land. This dual existence is most vividly exemplified by frogs and toads, whose journey from egg to adult involves a dramatic metamorphosis. Eggs are laid in water, where they hatch into tadpoles—aquatic larvae equipped with gills for breathing and tails for swimming. This aquatic phase allows them to exploit the rich resources of ponds and streams, feeding on algae and detritus while avoiding many terrestrial predators.

As tadpoles grow, they undergo a remarkable transformation. Legs develop, lungs replace gills, and the tail is absorbed, preparing them for life on land. This metamorphosis is a testament to the adaptability of amphibians, enabling them to exploit two distinct ecological niches. Once on land, adult frogs and toads become voracious predators, using their long, sticky tongues to capture insects and other small prey. Their permeable skin, while a vulnerability, also serves as an additional respiratory surface, allowing them to absorb oxygen from the air or water—a crucial adaptation for survival in diverse habitats.

Salamanders and newts, other members of the amphibian family, offer further insight into the diversity of dual life strategies. Some species, like the axolotl, retain their aquatic larval form throughout life, a condition known as neoteny. This adaptation allows them to remain in stable aquatic environments while avoiding the hazards of terrestrial life. Others, such as the spotted salamander, migrate to vernal pools to breed, utilizing temporary aquatic habitats that provide a safe haven for their young.

The ability to exploit both aquatic and terrestrial environments has equipped amphibians with a range of survival strategies. Their permeable skin, while advantageous for respiration, also poses challenges, as it leaves them susceptible to dehydration and environmental toxins. To mitigate these risks, many amphibians have developed behavioral adaptations, such as remaining in moist environments or becoming nocturnal to avoid the drying effects of the sun. Some species, like the desert-dwelling spadefoot toad, have evolved the ability to burrow underground and enter a state of dormancy during periods of drought, emerging only when conditions are favorable.

Amphibians also exhibit a variety of reproductive strategies that enhance their chances of survival across different environments. While many species lay their eggs in water, others have adapted to terrestrial breeding. The marsupial frog, for instance, carries its eggs in a pouch on its back, providing protection and a moist environment for development. Similarly, the male Darwin's frog guards its eggs by swallowing them, allowing them to develop in its vocal sac—a unique adaptation that ensures the safety of the young in a terrestrial setting.

The coloration and markings of amphibians often serve as a testament to their dual life strategies. Many species exhibit cryptic coloration that allows them to blend into their surroundings, avoiding detection by predators. The green tree frog, with its vibrant color, camouflages itself among leaves, while the mottled skin of the common toad helps it remain inconspicuous on the forest floor. Some amphibians, like the poison dart frog, flaunt bright colors as a warning to potential predators, advertising their toxicity and deterring attacks.

Despite their remarkable adaptations, amphibians are facing unprecedented challenges in the modern world. Habitat destruction, pollution, climate change, and disease have contributed to a global decline in amphibian populations. Their permeable skin makes them particularly vulnerable to pollutants and pathogens, while changes in temperature and moisture levels can disrupt their breeding and survival. Conservation efforts are critical to preserving these unique creatures and the ecosystems they inhabit.

Understanding the dual life strategies of amphibians provides valuable insights into the complexity and resilience of life. Their ability to adapt to both water and land underscores the importance of flexibility in evolution, allowing them to exploit diverse environments and resources. As we continue to study these amphibious wonders, we gain a deeper appreciation for the evolutionary processes that have shaped them and the delicate balance that sustains their existence.

Insect Innovations The Tiny Titans of the Land

Insects, the most diverse and numerous group of animals on the planet, are true marvels of adaptation and innovation. These tiny titans have colonized virtually every terrestrial habitat, from the scorching sands of deserts to the lush foliage of rainforests. Their success is due to an extraordinary array of physical and behavioral adaptations that allow them to exploit a wide range of ecological niches and withstand environmental pressures.

The exoskeleton is one of the most defining features of insects. This rigid outer shell, composed of chitin, serves multiple functions: it provides protection against predators and environmental hazards, prevents desiccation in dry climates, and acts as a support structure for muscle attachment. The exoskeleton's segmented design allows for flexibility and mobility, enabling insects to move with agility and precision. It also facilitates growth through a process known as molting, where the insect sheds its old exoskeleton and forms a new, larger one, accommodating their developmental stages.

Insects exhibit a vast array of morphological adaptations, each tailored to their specific lifestyle and habitat. The diversity of mouthparts among insects is a prime example, reflecting their varied diets and feeding strategies. Butterflies and moths possess a long, coiled proboscis, ideal for sipping nectar from flowers, while the formidable mandibles of ants and beetles are adapted for biting and chewing. Mosquitoes have evolved specialized mouthparts to pierce skin and siphon blood, illustrating the precision of insect adaptations in meeting their nutritional needs.

The ability to fly is another remarkable innovation that has contributed to the success of many insect species. Wings, whether membranous like those of dragonflies or hardened like those of beetles, provide insects with unparalleled mobility, enabling them to escape predators, find food, and disperse to new territories. The intricate wing patterns of butterflies and moths serve additional functions, such as camouflage, mate attraction, and warning signals to potential predators, showcasing the multifaceted role of wings in insect life.

Insects have also developed sophisticated sensory systems that allow them to perceive and respond to their environment with remarkable acuity. Compound eyes, composed of numerous individual lenses, provide a wide field of vision and detect movement with great efficiency. Antennae serve as versatile sensory organs, detecting chemical signals, temperature changes, and humidity levels. The ability to sense pheromones, chemical signals used for communication, is particularly refined in insects like ants and bees, facilitating complex social interactions and coordination within colonies.

Social behavior in insects is a testament to their innovative adaptations. Eusocial insects, such as bees, ants, and termites, live in highly organized colonies that function as a single entity. Division of labor, where individuals specialize in specific roles such as foraging, defense, or reproduction, enhances the efficiency and survival of the colony. The intricate communication systems of these insects, often based on pheromones or tactile signals, ensure coordination and cohesion within the group. The construction of elaborate nests and hives, using materials like wax or soil, further exemplifies the ingenuity of social insects in creating and maintaining complex living environments.

Camouflage and mimicry are among the most striking adaptations in insects, providing them with vital defense mechanisms against predators. The leaf insect, with its uncanny resemblance to a leaf, and the stick insect, which mimics twigs, are masters of disguise, blending seamlessly into their surroundings. Some insects, like the viceroy butterfly, engage in mimicry, adopting the appearance of unpalatable species to deter predators. These adaptations highlight the evolutionary arms race between insects and their predators, driving the development of increasingly sophisticated survival strategies.

The reproductive strategies of insects are as diverse as their forms, enabling them to exploit a wide range of habitats and resources. Some insects, like the praying mantis, engage in elaborate courtship rituals that ensure successful mating, while others, such as aphids, employ parthenogenesis, reproducing without fertilization to rapidly increase their numbers. Oviposition, the laying of eggs, is often highly specialized, with insects depositing eggs in locations that provide optimal conditions for the development of their offspring. The adaptability of reproductive strategies ensures the persistence of insect populations across diverse environments.

Insects also play crucial ecological roles, acting as pollinators, decomposers, and prey for other animals. Pollinators like bees, butterflies, and beetles facilitate the reproduction of flowering plants, supporting biodiversity and agriculture. Decomposers, including various beetles and flies, break down organic matter, recycling nutrients and maintaining ecosystem health. The presence of insects in food webs provides a vital link between primary producers and higher trophic levels, illustrating their importance in sustaining ecological balance.

Despite their small size, insects face significant challenges in the modern world. Habitat loss, pesticide use, and climate change pose threats to insect populations, with potential repercussions for the ecosystems they support. Conservation efforts aimed at preserving insect diversity and their habitats are essential for maintaining ecological stability and ensuring the continued provision of ecosystem services.

The Art of Camouflage Blending in to Survive

In the intricate dance of survival, camouflage stands as one of nature's most captivating and effective strategies. The art of blending into one's surroundings is an evolutionary masterpiece, enabling countless species to evade predators, ambush prey, and thrive in hostile environments. This remarkable adaptation manifests in myriad forms across the animal kingdom, showcasing the creativity and ingenuity of life on Earth.

Camouflage, at its core, is about deception. It allows organisms to become invisible or misleadingly visible, depending on their ecological roles. Predators and prey alike employ this tactic, each with distinct objectives but utilizing similar principles to achieve them. For many animals, survival hinges on the ability to vanish seamlessly into their environments, a feat achieved through coloration, patterning, and behavior.

The polar bear, a master of Arctic camouflage, exemplifies how coloration can be a crucial survival tool. Its white fur blends effortlessly with the snow and ice, concealing the bear from unsuspecting seals. This natural disguise enables the bear to approach its prey undetected, highlighting the predatory advantage of camouflage. In contrast, animals like the snowshoe hare change their coat color with the seasons, morphing from brown in summer to white in winter. This seasonal adaptation ensures that they remain hidden from predators year-round, illustrating the prey's use of camouflage to avoid detection.

Patterning is another key element of camouflage, often serving to disrupt an animal's outline and make it less recognizable. The stripes of a zebra, for example, create a confusing visual effect that makes it difficult for predators to single out an individual from the herd. Similarly, the spots on a leopard's coat mimic the dappled sunlight filtering through the forest canopy, allowing it to stalk prey with stealth and precision. These patterns, though seemingly random, are meticulously crafted by evolution to enhance survival through concealment.

Mimicry, a form of camouflage where one species evolves to resemble another, adds another layer of complexity to this survival strategy. The harmless hawk moth caterpillar, when threatened, inflates its body to mimic the appearance of a snake, complete with convincing eyespots. This startling transformation deters would-be predators, providing a clear example of how mimicry can be a powerful deterrent. Similarly, the viceroy butterfly mimics the toxic monarch butterfly, fooling predators into thinking it is equally unpalatable and thus avoiding predation.

Behavioral adaptations often accompany physical camouflage, enhancing its effectiveness. The common cuttlefish, renowned for its ability to change color and texture, can also mimic the movements of other sea creatures or remain motionless among rocks and sand. This dynamic form of camouflage allows the cuttlefish to evade predators and surprise prey, showcasing the intricate interplay between appearance and behavior in the art of concealment. In the insect world, the leaf insect takes mimicry to new heights by swaying gently to mimic the movement of leaves in the breeze, avoiding detection by predators.

Environmental context plays a crucial role in the success of camouflage. An animal's ability to blend in is highly dependent on the habitat it occupies. The rock ptarmigan, for instance, matches its surroundings by changing its plumage to mirror the rocky, snow-covered terrain it inhabits. This adaptation is a testament to the specificity with which camouflage evolves, fine-tuned to the unique conditions of an organism's environment.

While camouflage is a boon for survival, it is not without its challenges. Predators have evolved sharp senses and strategies to counteract the effects of camouflage, leading to an ongoing evolutionary arms race. The keen eyesight of birds of prey, for example, can penetrate the disguises of many camouflaged creatures, while the acute sense of smell in canines can detect hidden prey. This dynamic interplay between camouflage and detection drives the continuous refinement of these adaptations, resulting in an ever-evolving landscape of survival strategies. activities pose new challenges to the effectiveness of natural camouflage. Habitat destruction, climate change, and pollution alter the environments that species have adapted to over millennia, potentially rendering their camouflage ineffective. Animals that rely on specific backgrounds for concealment may find themselves increasingly vulnerable as their habitats change or disappear. Conservation efforts that prioritize habitat preservation are crucial in maintaining the delicate balance that allows camouflage to function as a survival mechanism.

The art of camouflage extends beyond the animal kingdom, influencing human culture and technology. Military applications have long drawn inspiration from nature, employing camouflage patterns to conceal personnel and equipment. The study of natural camouflage informs advances in materials science, robotics, and design, demonstrating how deeply interconnected human innovation and biological adaptation can be.

In exploring the art of camouflage, we gain insight into the intricate strategies that have evolved to ensure survival in a competitive world. The diversity of camouflage techniques reflects the adaptability and resilience of life, offering a window into the complex interactions between organisms and their environments. By understanding and appreciating these natural wonders, we can foster a deeper connection to the natural world and inspire efforts to preserve the ecosystems that sustain this delicate dance of survival.

Chapter 3

Aerial Acrobats Life in the Skies

The Mechanics of Flight Wings and Feathers

Flight, a marvel of nature, has captivated human imagination for centuries. Among the diverse creatures that have conquered the skies, birds stand as paragons of aerial mastery, their wings and feathers perfectly engineered for flight. The mechanics of flight involve a complex interplay of anatomy, physics, and behavior, each component crucial to the remarkable ability to soar through the air with grace and precision.

At the heart of avian flight lies the wing, a structure that combines strength with flexibility. The wing's primary function is to generate lift, the upward force that counteracts gravity and keeps the bird aloft. To achieve this, the wing must be shaped to create a pressure differential between its upper and lower surfaces. This shape is known as an airfoil, and it is essential for efficient flight. As air flows over the curved upper surface of the wing, it travels faster than the air beneath, resulting in lower pressure above the wing and higher pressure below, thus generating lift.

The skeletal structure of a bird's wing is both lightweight and robust, optimized for flight. The bones are hollow and filled with air sacs, reducing weight without sacrificing strength. The humerus, radius, and ulna form the main framework, with the wrist and finger bones supporting the primary and secondary feathers. These feathers are crucial for flight, each playing a specific role in lift, thrust, and maneuverability. The primary feathers, attached to the hand, are responsible for propulsion and steering, while the secondary feathers, attached to the forearm, provide lift.

Feathers, the defining feature of birds, are marvels of natural engineering. Composed of keratin, they are lightweight yet durable, designed to withstand the rigors of flight. Each feather consists of a central shaft, or rachis, with barbs extending from either side. These barbs interlock with tiny hooks called barbules, creating a smooth, aerodynamic surface. This intricate structure allows feathers to provide the necessary lift and thrust while minimizing air resistance.

The arrangement and condition of feathers are critical for effective flight. Birds maintain their feathers through preening, a behavior that involves using their beaks to align the barbs and remove dirt and parasites. Preening also distributes oils from a gland near the base of the tail, which waterproofs the feathers and maintains their flexibility. Molting, the periodic shedding and replacement of feathers, ensures that birds maintain optimal flight capabilities by replacing worn or damaged feathers with new ones.

The mechanics of flight extend beyond the physical structure of wings and feathers to include the intricate movements and behaviors that enable birds to navigate the sky. Flapping flight, the most common form of avian locomotion, involves a coordinated sequence of wing beats that generate both lift and thrust. During the downstroke, the wing moves downward and forward, creating lift and propelling the bird forward. The upstroke, in contrast, is more passive, with the wing partially folded to reduce air resistance.

Soaring and gliding are energy-efficient forms of flight that take advantage of environmental conditions to maintain altitude with minimal effort. Soaring birds, such as eagles and vultures, utilize thermal updrafts—columns of rising warm air—to gain altitude without flapping their wings. Gliding involves descending at an angle, using gravity to maintain forward momentum while minimizing energy expenditure. These flight strategies exemplify the adaptability of birds to various ecological niches and environmental conditions.

Maneuverability is another critical aspect of flight, essential for avoiding obstacles, capturing prey, and escaping predators. Birds achieve this through precise control of wing shape and position, adjusting the angle and curvature of their wings to change direction swiftly. The tail also plays a vital role in steering and stability, acting as a rudder to guide the bird's movements.

The evolution of flight in birds is a testament to the power of natural selection, shaping their anatomy and behavior to optimize aerial prowess. This evolutionary process has resulted in a stunning diversity of flight adaptations, from the rapid wing beats of hummingbirds to the broad, soaring wings of albatrosses. Each species has evolved a unique set of flight characteristics tailored to its ecological niche and lifestyle.

Flight has not only shaped the anatomy and behavior of birds but has also influenced their ecology and distribution. The ability to fly allows birds to exploit a wide range of habitats, migrate across continents, and access resources unavailable to terrestrial animals. This has contributed to the global success and diversity of avian species, making them one of the most widespread and varied groups of vertebrates.

While birds are the most iconic fliers, other animals have also evolved the ability to take to the skies. Bats, the only mammals capable of sustained flight, possess wings formed by a membrane of skin stretched between elongated fingers. Insects, too, have independently evolved flight, with wings that operate on different principles but achieve similar outcomes. These diverse adaptations highlight the convergent evolution of flight, demonstrating that the mechanics of taking to the air can arise from different evolutionary pathways.

The study of flight mechanics offers valuable insights into the principles of aerodynamics and biomechanics, informing advances in aviation and engineering. By understanding the intricacies of avian flight, researchers can develop more efficient aircraft designs, improve wind energy technology, and explore new possibilities in robotics. The elegance and efficiency of natural flight continue to inspire innovation, bridging the gap between biology and technology.

Avian Adaptations Navigating the Air Currents

The skies, an expansive realm of endless possibilities, have been mastered by birds through an array of astonishing adaptations. These creatures, whose ancestors took to the air millions of years ago, have honed their abilities to navigate the air currents with precision and grace. Understanding avian adaptations not only reveals the secrets of their flight but also highlights the intricate relationship between form, function, and environment.

Birds possess a suite of physical traits that equip them for the rigors of flight. Chief among these is the lightweight skeletal structure, a marvel of evolutionary engineering. Hollow bones reduce body weight without compromising strength, allowing for efficient energy use during flight. The fusion of certain bones, such as the collarbone forming the furcula, provides additional structural support and aids in the distribution of stress during wing beats.

The avian respiratory system is another critical adaptation, uniquely designed to meet the high oxygen demands of flight. Unlike mammals, birds have a series of air sacs connected to their lungs, facilitating a continuous flow of air and ensuring that oxygen exchange occurs both during inhalation and exhalation. This efficient system maximizes oxygen uptake, allowing birds to sustain prolonged periods of activity and traverse vast distances during migration.

Feathers, the quintessential feature of birds, play a multifaceted role in flight adaptation. Composed of keratin, feathers are lightweight yet durable, providing the necessary lift and thrust while maintaining aerodynamic efficiency. The arrangement of feathers on the wings creates an airfoil, a shape that generates lift by manipulating air pressure. Tail feathers aid in steering and braking, while body feathers streamline the bird's profile, reducing drag.

The diversity of wing shapes and sizes among birds reflects the various ecological niches they occupy. Long, narrow wings, like those of albatrosses, are adapted for soaring over open oceans, taking advantage of wind currents to minimize energy expenditure. In contrast, the short, rounded wings of sparrows and finches are suited for rapid takeoffs and agile maneuvers in dense vegetation. These variations illustrate the adaptability of avian wing morphology to specific environments and lifestyles.

Behavioral adaptations further enhance a bird's ability to navigate the air currents. Migratory species, such as swallows and geese, have evolved innate abilities to orient themselves using the sun, stars, and Earth's magnetic field. These navigational skills enable them to undertake epic journeys across continents, exploiting seasonal resources and favorable weather patterns. The timing and routes of migration are finely tuned to coincide with the availability of food and suitable breeding grounds, demonstrating the intricate connection between behavior and environmental cues.

Social behaviors also play a role in avian navigation. Many birds travel in flocks, a strategy that offers several advantages. Flocking can reduce individual energy expenditure by allowing birds to take turns leading and drafting, similar to cyclists in a peloton. It also provides safety in numbers, reducing the risk of predation. The coordination and communication required for flocking highlight the complex social structures that underpin avian life.

Birds have developed specialized feeding adaptations that complement their flight capabilities. The shape and structure of a bird's beak are closely linked to its diet and feeding habits. Hummingbirds, with their long, slender bills, are perfectly equipped to extract nectar from flowers, while the hooked beak of a hawk is designed for tearing flesh. These adaptations illustrate the relationship between form and function, where the demands of feeding drive the evolution of specific traits.

The evolution of sensory adaptations has further enhanced the ability of birds to navigate and thrive in their environments. Keen eyesight, a hallmark of many bird species, allows for the detection of prey and predators from great distances. Raptors, such as eagles and hawks, possess binocular vision and a high density of photoreceptor cells, providing them with exceptional visual acuity. In contrast, nocturnal birds like owls have adapted to low-light conditions with large eyes and enhanced night vision, enabling them to hunt effectively under the cover of darkness.

Vocalizations and auditory capabilities also play a vital role in avian life. Birds use calls and songs for communication, mate attraction, and territory defense. The ability to produce and interpret a wide range of sounds is facilitated by the syrinx, a unique vocal organ located at the base of the trachea. This adaptation allows for complex vocalizations that are integral to social interactions and reproductive success.

The interplay between avian adaptations and environmental factors is a dynamic process, driven by the pressures of natural selection. As habitats change and new challenges arise, birds continue to evolve, refining their adaptations to maintain their mastery of the skies. This ongoing evolution underscores the resilience and adaptability of avian species, testament to their enduring success across the globe.

In the face of modern threats such as habitat loss, climate change, and pollution, the adaptability of birds is being tested. Conservation efforts aimed at preserving critical habitats and mitigating human impacts are essential for ensuring the survival of these remarkable creatures. By protecting the ecosystems that support avian life, we safeguard the intricate web of interactions that sustain biodiversity and ecological balance.

The Role of Migration in Survival

Migration, a natural phenomenon of epic proportions, is a critical survival strategy adopted by countless species around the globe. This instinctual journey, often spanning thousands of miles, is driven by the need to find food, suitable breeding grounds, and favorable living conditions. The role of migration in survival is a testament to the resilience and adaptability of life on Earth, showcasing the intricate balance between biology and environment.

For many species, migration is a response to the changing availability of resources. Seasonal variations, such as the onset of winter or the dry season, can drastically alter the abundance of food and water in an area. In temperate regions, where harsh winters limit food availability, many bird species embark on long journeys to warmer climates. The Arctic tern, for instance, undertakes one of the longest migrations in the animal kingdom, traveling from its Arctic breeding grounds to the Antarctic and back each year. This incredible journey ensures access to continuous daylight and abundant feeding opportunities, highlighting how migration can mitigate the challenges posed by seasonal resource fluctuations.

The role of migration extends beyond mere survival; it is also crucial for successful reproduction. Many animals migrate to specific breeding grounds that provide optimal conditions for raising offspring. The great wildebeest migration in Africa, for example, sees millions of wildebeest, zebras, and other herbivores journey across the Serengeti and Maasai Mara in search of fresh grazing lands and water. This migration is timed to coincide with the birth of calves, ensuring that the young have access to the resources they need for growth and development. By moving to areas with fewer predators and plentiful food, these animals increase the chances of survival for their offspring.

Migration is not limited to terrestrial animals; marine species also undertake vast journeys. The humpback whale, known for its haunting songs and acrobatic displays, migrates between feeding and breeding grounds. These magnificent creatures travel from nutrient-rich polar waters, where they feed during the summer, to tropical or subtropical waters for breeding in the winter. This migration minimizes the risk to vulnerable calves from predators and harsh conditions, illustrating the protective role of migration in marine environments.

Navigational skills are paramount for successful migration. Animals employ a variety of methods to orient themselves and stay on course. Birds, for instance, use a combination of celestial cues, Earth's magnetic field, and landmarks to navigate. The monarch butterfly, famous for its multigenerational migration from North America to central Mexico, relies on the position of the sun and an internal circadian clock to guide its journey. These sophisticated navigational abilities are a testament to the evolutionary pressures that have shaped migratory behavior.

While migration offers numerous benefits, it is fraught with challenges and risks. The physical demands of long-distance travel can be immense, requiring significant energy reserves and endurance. Many animals prepare for migration by accumulating fat stores, which serve as fuel for the journey. The bar-tailed godwit, a shorebird, holds the record for the longest non-stop flight, traveling over 7,000 miles from Alaska to New Zealand without pausing to rest or feed. This remarkable feat underscores the endurance and resilience required for successful migration.

Predation is another significant threat during migration. The concentration of animals in specific areas or along migratory routes can attract predators, leading to increased mortality rates. The salmon run, an iconic migratory event, draws numerous predators, including bears and birds of prey, to the rivers where salmon return to spawn. While this presents a risk to individual fish, the sheer number of migrating salmon ensures that enough survive to reproduce and sustain the population. activities pose additional challenges to migratory species. Habitat destruction, climate change, and pollution can disrupt migratory routes and degrade critical stopover sites. Many migratory birds rely on wetlands and other habitats for resting and refueling during their journeys. The loss of these habitats can have devastating effects on bird populations, emphasizing the need for conservation efforts that prioritize the protection of migratory corridors and stopover sites.

Climate change presents a particularly complex challenge for migratory species. Shifts in temperature and weather patterns can alter the timing of resource availability, leading to mismatches between migration schedules and the conditions animals depend on. Early springs, for example, may cause plants to bloom before migratory pollinators arrive, disrupting ecological relationships that have evolved over millennia. Understanding and addressing these impacts is essential for ensuring the continued survival of migratory species.

The cultural and ecological significance of migration extends beyond the animal kingdom. Human societies have long been influenced by migratory patterns, with many cultures celebrating these natural events through festivals and traditions. The return of migratory birds in spring, for instance, is often seen as a symbol of renewal and hope. Additionally, migratory species play vital roles in ecosystems as pollinators, seed dispersers, and prey, contributing to biodiversity and ecological balance.

Efforts to conserve migratory species require international cooperation, as these animals often traverse multiple countries and continents. Treaties such as the Convention on Migratory Species aim to protect migratory routes and habitats, ensuring that these incredible journeys can continue for generations to come. By fostering collaboration and raising awareness, we can work towards a future where migratory species thrive in harmony with human development.

Insect Flyers Masters of Aerial Maneuvers

Insect flyers, those diminutive masters of the sky, have captivated scientists and nature enthusiasts alike with their astonishing aerial abilities. Despite their small size, insects like bees, dragonflies, and butterflies execute complex maneuvers with precision and efficiency that rival the most advanced aircraft. These creatures have evolved a plethora of adaptations that allow them not only to survive but to thrive in the air, making them some of the most successful and diverse animals on the planet.

The mechanics of insect flight are a marvel of evolutionary engineering. Unlike birds, whose wings are rigid and operate on a flapping motion, insect wings are flexible and can twist, tilt, and rotate to produce lift and thrust. This flexibility allows insects to hover, dart, and change direction in the blink of an eye, enabling them to evade predators, catch prey, and navigate complex environments with ease.

Dragonflies, for instance, are renowned for their incredible agility and speed. Their two pairs of wings can beat independently, allowing them to perform acrobatic feats such as flying backward, hovering in place, and making sharp turns. This capability is due to a direct flight muscle system, where muscles attach directly to the wings, providing precise control over wing movements. Dragonflies are also capable of sustained flight, making them formidable hunters that can catch prey mid-air with astonishing accuracy.

The flight of bees offers another fascinating example of insect aerial prowess. Bees are vital pollinators, and their ability to fly efficiently is crucial for their role in ecosystems. Their wings operate on an indirect flight muscle system, where the muscles attach to the thorax rather than the wings themselves. This arrangement allows for rapid wing beats, sometimes exceeding 200 beats per second, enabling bees to hover and maneuver with exceptional dexterity. The wing motion of bees creates vortices that generate lift, a mechanism that has intrigued scientists and inspired studies into aerodynamics.

Butterflies, with their strikingly patterned wings, demonstrate a different approach to flight. Their wings are larger and flimsier than those of other insects, resulting in a more erratic flight pattern. This seemingly inefficient flight actually serves a purpose: it makes them unpredictable and harder for predators to capture. Butterflies are also capable of long-distance migrations, such as the iconic journey of the monarch butterfly, which travels thousands of miles from North America to central Mexico. This migration showcases their endurance and the role of flight in their survival strategy.

Insect wings are not just tools for locomotion; they are masterpieces of structural design. The wings are composed of a thin membrane stretched over a network of veins that provide support and flexibility. This structure allows for the absorption of impact and resistance to damage, ensuring that insects can continue to fly even after sustaining minor injuries. The lightweight and efficient design of insect wings is a testament to the power of natural selection in optimizing flight capabilities.

Sensory adaptations play a crucial role in the success of insect flyers. Compound eyes, composed of numerous tiny lenses, provide insects with a wide field of view and the ability to detect fast movements. This visual acuity is essential for navigating their environment, avoiding obstacles, and identifying food sources. In addition to vision, insects rely on their antennae for detecting chemical cues in the air, which guide them to flowers, mates, and suitable habitats. These sensory adaptations are integral to the precision and effectiveness of insect flight.

The ecological impact of insect flyers is profound. As pollinators, insects like bees and butterflies are essential for the reproduction of flowering plants, contributing to biodiversity and food production. Their role in pollination supports ecosystems and human agriculture, highlighting the interconnectedness of life. Predatory insects, such as dragonflies, help control pest populations, maintaining ecological balance. The flight capabilities of insects enable them to fulfill these crucial roles, underscoring their importance in natural systems. activities, however, pose significant threats to insect populations. Habitat loss, pesticide use, and climate change are leading to declines in insect numbers, with potentially devastating consequences for ecosystems and food security. Conservation efforts that focus on preserving habitats and reducing chemical use are vital for protecting insect populations and ensuring the continuation of their ecological roles.

The study of insect flight has also inspired technological advancements. The principles of insect flight mechanics have been applied to the development of micro aerial vehicles (MAVs), small drones designed for surveillance, environmental monitoring, and search and rescue operations. By mimicking the flight patterns and wing structures of insects, engineers have created MAVs that can hover, navigate tight spaces, and perform complex maneuvers, demonstrating the potential for biomimicry in technological innovation.

Nocturnal Navigators Bats and Their Unique Adaptations

In the quiet embrace of the night, a remarkable group of creatures takes to the skies, navigating the darkness with an extraordinary array of adaptations. Bats, the only mammals capable of sustained flight, have mastered the art of nocturnal navigation, thriving in an environment where others might struggle to survive. Their unique adaptations not only allow them to maneuver through the night with uncanny precision but also play a crucial role in maintaining ecological balance.

The anatomy of a bat's wing is a marvel of evolutionary design. Unlike birds, whose wings are composed of feathers, bat wings are formed by a thin membrane of skin stretched over elongated fingers. This structure grants bats exceptional control over their flight, enabling them to execute agile maneuvers and hover in place. The flexibility of the wing membrane also allows for a wide range of motion, making bats adept at capturing insects on the wing and navigating through dense foliage.

Bats possess an unparalleled ability to navigate in complete darkness, a skill that is largely attributed to their sophisticated echolocation system. Echolocation involves emitting high-frequency sound waves that bounce off objects and return as echoes, which bats interpret to construct a mental map of their surroundings. This sonar-like ability enables bats to detect prey, avoid obstacles, and orient themselves in the dark. The precision of echolocation is such that some bats can discern the size, shape, and texture of objects, allowing them to target specific prey even in pitch-black conditions.

The diversity of bat species is reflected in the variety of echolocation strategies they employ. Some bats, like the common pipistrelle, emit short, high-pitched calls that provide detailed information about their immediate surroundings, making them adept at hunting small insects in cluttered environments.

Others, such as the greater bulldog bat, use lower frequency calls that travel further, allowing them to detect prey over open water. These adaptations demonstrate the versatility of echolocation and its importance in the survival of bats across different habitats.

Bats are not only skilled navigators but also play vital roles in ecosystems. As insectivores, they help control pest populations, reducing the need for chemical pesticides and benefiting agriculture. Fruit-eating bats, on the other hand, are important pollinators and seed dispersers, contributing to the regeneration of forests and the maintenance of plant diversity. The ecological services provided by bats underscore their significance in natural systems and highlight the interconnectedness of life.

The ability of bats to thrive in the night is further enhanced by their acute sensory adaptations. In addition to echolocation, many bats have excellent hearing, allowing them to detect the faintest sounds. This sensitivity is crucial for communication within colonies and for locating prey. Some species, like the vampire bat, have evolved heat-sensitive receptors on their noses that help them detect the body heat of their prey, illustrating the remarkable diversity of sensory adaptations among bats.

Despite their ecological importance, bats face numerous threats that jeopardize their survival. Habitat destruction, climate change, and diseases such as white-nose syndrome have led to declines in bat populations worldwide. White-nose syndrome, caused by a fungal pathogen, has decimated bat colonies in North America, highlighting the vulnerability of these creatures to environmental changes. Conservation efforts are essential to protect bat habitats, mitigate the impacts of human activities, and ensure the survival of these nocturnal navigators.

The study of bat adaptations has inspired technological advancements, particularly in the field of sonar and radar technology. By mimicking the echolocation techniques of bats, engineers have developed systems with applications in navigation, surveillance, and even medical imaging. These innovations demonstrate the potential for biomimicry to drive technological progress and solve complex challenges.

Bats, with their unique adaptations and ecological roles, serve as a reminder of the ingenuity and diversity of life on Earth. Their mastery of nocturnal navigation is a testament to the power of evolution and the intricate balance that sustains the natural world. As we continue to explore and understand the world of bats, we gain valuable insights into the complexities of ecosystems and the importance of preserving biodiversity.

Chapter 4

Aquatic Marvels Thriving Beneath the Waves

Fish Forms and Functions Adaptations for Aquatic Life

Beneath the shimmering surface of rivers, lakes, and oceans lies a world teeming with diverse and fascinating life forms. Among them, fish have evolved an astounding array of adaptations that enable them to thrive in the aquatic realm. Their forms and functions are intricately linked with their environments, showcasing the remarkable power of evolution to shape life in water.

The body shape of a fish is a primary adaptation that reflects its lifestyle and habitat. Streamlined, torpedo-shaped bodies are common among fast-swimming fish like tuna and mackerel, allowing them to cut through water with minimal resistance. This hydrodynamic design is crucial for species that rely on speed and agility to catch prey or avoid predators. In contrast, fish like angelfish and butterflyfish, which inhabit coral reefs, have laterally compressed bodies that enable them to maneuver easily through narrow crevices and complex structures.

The diversity of fin structures among fish also highlights the relationship between form and function. Fins provide stability, propulsion, and steering capabilities, facilitating a wide range of movements. The pectoral fins of wrasses, for example, are adapted for precise control and rapid turns, essential for navigating the intricate reef environment. The wing-like pectoral fins of the flying fish allow it to glide above the water's surface, evading predators with remarkable efficiency. These specialized adaptations illustrate the evolutionary innovations that have arisen to meet the demands of different aquatic lifestyles.

Gills are a defining feature of fish, enabling them to extract oxygen from water. The structure of gills consists of thin filaments covered with lamellae, which provide a large surface area for gas exchange. As water flows over the gills, oxygen diffuses into the blood while carbon dioxide is expelled. This efficient respiratory system is vital for sustaining the high metabolic rates of active fish. In some species, such as the labyrinth fish, accessory breathing structures have evolved to allow them to survive in oxygen-poor environments by gulping air at the water's surface.

The scales of fish serve as protective armor, shielding them from physical damage and parasites. The composition and arrangement of scales vary among species, reflecting different ecological and behavioral adaptations. Cycloid and ctenoid scales, found in most bony fish, are smooth and overlapping, providing flexibility and reducing drag. In contrast, the ganoid scales of gar are thick and diamond-shaped, offering robust protection. These variations in scale structure highlight the adaptability of fish to diverse environments and threats.

Sensory adaptations play a crucial role in the survival of fish, enabling them to detect changes in their environment and respond effectively. The lateral line system, a series of sensory cells along the sides of the body, allows fish to sense vibrations and movements in the water. This adaptation is particularly important for schooling fish, such as herring, which rely on the lateral line to maintain coordinated group movements and avoid predators. Additionally, many fish possess acute vision and can perceive a wide range of colors, aiding in the identification of prey, mates, and rivals.

Some fish have evolved specialized adaptations for feeding, reflecting the diversity of diets and ecological niches occupied by these animals. The elongated jaws of the swordfish and billfish, for instance, are adapted for slashing through schools of fish, while the suction-feeding mechanism of the anglerfish allows it to engulf prey with lightning speed. Herbivorous fish, like the parrotfish, have beak-like jaws for scraping algae from coral surfaces. These feeding adaptations demonstrate the intricate relationship between form, function, and ecological role.

Reproductive strategies among fish are as varied as their forms and functions, with adaptations that enhance the chances of survival for offspring. Many fish engage in elaborate courtship displays to attract mates, while others rely on external fertilization, releasing eggs and sperm into the water. Some species, such as the seahorse, exhibit unique parental care, with males carrying and protecting developing embryos in a specialized pouch. These reproductive adaptations reflect the diverse strategies fish employ to ensure the continuation of their species.

The ability of fish to adapt to a wide range of environmental conditions is evident in their distribution across the globe, from the icy waters of the Arctic to the warm, tropical seas. Some fish, like the Arctic char, have antifreeze proteins in their blood, allowing them to survive in frigid temperatures. Others, such as the lungfish, can aestivate during dry periods, burrowing into the mud and breathing air until water returns. These physiological adaptations highlight the resilience and versatility of fish in the face of environmental challenges. activities, however, pose significant threats to fish populations and their habitats. Overfishing, pollution, and habitat destruction have led to declines in many fish species, with far-reaching consequences for ecosystems and human societies. Conservation efforts that focus on sustainable fishing practices, habitat restoration, and pollution reduction are critical for protecting fish diversity and ensuring the health of aquatic ecosystems.

The study of fish forms and functions provides valuable insights into the complexities of life in water, illustrating the dynamic interplay between organisms and their environments. By understanding the adaptations that enable fish to thrive, we can appreciate the intricate web of interactions that sustain aquatic ecosystems and the importance of preserving these vital habitats.

Marine Mammals Breathing Underwater

The vast expanse of the ocean is home to some of the most enigmatic and captivating creatures on Earth: marine mammals. These animals, which include whales, dolphins, seals, and manatees, are perfectly adapted to life in the water. Yet, despite their aquatic lifestyles, marine mammals are air-breathing creatures, an adaptation that poses unique challenges and has led to an array of fascinating evolutionary developments.

The primary challenge for marine mammals is the need to surface for air while spending extended periods underwater. This requirement has driven the evolution of remarkable physiological adaptations that allow them to efficiently manage their oxygen supply. One of the most notable adaptations is the ability to hold their breath for impressive durations. The sperm whale, for example, can dive to depths of over 3,000 meters and remain submerged for more than an hour. This feat is achieved through a combination of anatomical and physiological mechanisms that optimize oxygen storage and utilization.

Marine mammals have a higher concentration of myoglobin in their muscles compared to terrestrial mammals. Myoglobin is a protein that binds oxygen, allowing marine mammals to store large quantities of it in their muscles. This adaptation is crucial for sustaining muscle activity during long dives. Additionally, their blood contains a higher concentration of red blood cells, which enhances their capacity to transport oxygen throughout the body. These adaptations enable marine mammals to extend their dive times and explore the depths of the ocean with ease.

The circulatory system of marine mammals is also adapted to conserve oxygen during dives. They possess the ability to reduce blood flow to nonessential organs, directing oxygen-rich blood to vital organs such as the brain and heart. This physiological response, known as the dive reflex, is triggered by the cold water contacting the face and is a key factor in their ability to dive for extended periods. The dive reflex also includes a reduction in heart rate, a phenomenon known as bradycardia, which further conserves oxygen by slowing the metabolic rate.

Efficient breathing is another critical adaptation for marine mammals. Unlike terrestrial mammals, which typically inhale and exhale only a fraction of the air in their lungs with each breath, marine mammals exchange nearly all of the air in their lungs in a single breath. This rapid and complete exchange allows them to quickly replenish their oxygen supply at the surface before diving again. The blowhole, located on top of their heads, facilitates this process, enabling them to breathe without fully emerging from the water.

The structural design of the lungs and diaphragm in marine mammals also supports their diving lifestyle. Their lungs can collapse under high pressure, reducing the risk of nitrogen absorption and decompression sickness during deep dives. When a marine mammal dives, the pressure causes the alveoli, the tiny air sacs in the lungs, to collapse, pushing air into the more rigid airways. This adaptation minimizes nitrogen absorption and prevents the bends, a condition that can occur when nitrogen bubbles form in the blood upon resurfacing.

Communication and echolocation are additional adaptations that enhance the ability of marine mammals to thrive in their underwater environments.

Dolphins and some species of whales use echolocation to navigate, hunt, and communicate in the dark depths of the ocean. By emitting a series of clicks and listening for the returning echoes, these animals can detect objects, prey, and obstacles with astonishing precision. This adaptation is particularly valuable in murky waters where visibility is limited.

Social structures and behaviors are also integral to the survival of marine mammals. Many species, such as orcas and dolphins, live in complex social groups that cooperate in hunting, care for young, and protect one another from predators. These social bonds are reinforced through vocalizations, body language, and coordinated activities, enabling them to thrive in the challenging marine environment. The intelligence and social nature of marine mammals have long fascinated researchers and underscore the importance of social interactions in their survival strategies. activities, however, present significant threats to marine mammals. Overfishing, habitat destruction, pollution, and climate change have all contributed to the decline of many marine mammal populations. Additionally, noise pollution from ships and industrial activities can disrupt the communication and echolocation abilities of these animals, leading to disorientation and increased vulnerability. Conservation efforts that focus on protecting marine habitats, regulating human activities, and raising awareness are essential for ensuring the survival of marine mammals.

The study of marine mammals and their adaptations provides valuable insights into the complexities of life in the ocean. These animals, with their unique physiological and behavioral traits, demonstrate the incredible capacity of life to adapt to diverse and challenging environments. By understanding and appreciating the adaptations of marine mammals, we gain a deeper awareness of the delicate balance that sustains marine ecosystems and the importance of preserving these vital habitats.

The World of Coral Reefs Symbiosis and Survival

Coral reefs, often referred to as the "rainforests of the sea," are among the most diverse and vibrant ecosystems on the planet. These underwater wonderlands are teeming with life, from the smallest microorganisms to the largest marine predators. At the heart of coral reefs lies a complex web of symbiotic relationships that enable their survival and growth, creating an intricate balance that supports a vast array of species.

The foundation of coral reefs is built upon the mutualistic relationship between coral polyps and zooxanthellae, microscopic algae that reside within the tissues of the coral. These algae play a crucial role in the survival of coral reefs by performing photosynthesis, a process that converts sunlight into energy. In return, the coral provides the zooxanthellae with a protected environment and access to nutrients. This symbiotic relationship is a cornerstone of reef ecosystems, as the energy produced by the algae fuels the growth and calcification of coral, forming the intricate structures that define reefs.

The vibrant colors of coral reefs are a direct result of the zooxanthellae and their photosynthetic activity. These colors not only create breathtaking underwater landscapes but also serve as indicators of coral health. When corals experience stress, such as increased water temperatures or pollution, they may expel their symbiotic algae, leading to a phenomenon known as coral bleaching. This loss of color signifies a breakdown in the symbiotic relationship and can lead to the decline and death of coral if conditions do not improve.

Coral reefs are home to an astounding diversity of life, with thousands of species relying on them for food, shelter, and breeding grounds. Fish, invertebrates, and other marine organisms form intricate networks of interdependence within the reef ecosystem. Predatory fish, such as groupers and barracudas, regulate the populations of smaller fish, maintaining the balance of the food web. Herbivorous fish, like parrotfish and surgeonfish, play a crucial role in preventing algae overgrowth, which can smother coral and inhibit its growth. This dynamic interplay of species contributes to the resilience and productivity of coral reefs.

The structural complexity of coral reefs provides a multitude of habitats and niches for marine life. Crevices, overhangs, and coral branches offer refuge and breeding sites for various organisms, from tiny shrimp to larger predators. This diversity of habitats fosters high levels of biodiversity, making coral reefs hotspots for marine life. The intricate architecture of reefs also serves as a natural barrier against waves and storms, protecting coastlines and reducing erosion.

Despite their resilience, coral reefs face numerous threats that endanger their survival. Climate change, pollution, overfishing, and destructive fishing practices are among the most pressing challenges. Rising sea temperatures and ocean acidification, driven by climate change, can lead to coral bleaching and weaken the structural integrity of reefs. Pollution from agricultural runoff, sewage, and plastic waste can smother coral and disrupt the delicate balance of reef ecosystems.

Overfishing and destructive fishing practices, such as blast fishing and cyanide fishing, further exacerbate the vulnerability of coral reefs. These activities not only deplete fish populations but also damage the physical structure of reefs, reducing their ability to support diverse marine life. The loss of key species can have cascading effects throughout the ecosystem, disrupting the balance of the food web and hindering the recovery of coral reefs.

Conservation efforts are vital to protect and restore coral reefs, ensuring their continued survival and the myriad benefits they provide. Marine protected areas, sustainable fishing practices, and habitat restoration projects are essential components of reef conservation. By establishing protected zones, we can reduce human impacts and allow ecosystems to recover and thrive. Habitat restoration, including coral farming and transplantation, can help rebuild damaged reefs and promote biodiversity.

Community involvement and education are also critical in the conservation of coral reefs. Local communities play a key role in protecting reefs through sustainable resource management and stewardship. Educational programs that raise awareness about the importance of coral reefs and the threats they face can inspire action and foster a sense of responsibility for their preservation. By empowering communities and fostering collaborations between governments, NGOs, and researchers, we can work towards a sustainable future for coral reefs.

The world of coral reefs exemplifies the extraordinary complexity and beauty of nature's symbiotic relationships. These ecosystems are a testament to the power of collaboration and interdependence, where countless species coexist and thrive in harmony. As we deepen our understanding of coral reefs and their symbiosis, we gain valuable insights into the mechanisms that sustain life on Earth and the importance of preserving these vital ecosystems.

Ocean Giants The Adaptations of Whales and Sharks

The vast oceans are home to some of the most magnificent and awe-inspiring creatures on Earth: whales and sharks. These ocean giants have captivated human imagination for centuries, their sheer size and power evoking both wonder and respect. Despite their differences in taxonomy, whales and sharks share a remarkable ability to thrive in marine environments, thanks to a suite of specialized adaptations that have evolved over millions of years.

Whales, the gentle giants of the sea, belong to the order Cetacea and are divided into two subgroups: baleen whales and toothed whales. Baleen whales, such as the blue whale and humpback whale, are filter feeders. They possess baleen plates instead of teeth, which they use to strain krill and small fish from the water. This feeding adaptation allows them to efficiently exploit vast quantities of prey, supporting their enormous energy needs. The largest animal on the planet, the blue whale, can consume up to four tons of krill per day, demonstrating the efficiency of this feeding strategy.

The streamlined bodies of whales are perfectly adapted for life in the open ocean. Their fusiform shape reduces drag, enabling them to glide gracefully through water. The powerful tail flukes provide propulsion, while their pectoral fins offer stability and maneuverability. The blubber layer beneath their skin serves multiple purposes, providing insulation in cold waters, energy storage, and buoyancy. This combination of adaptations allows whales to undertake long migrations, traveling thousands of miles between feeding and breeding grounds.

Whales are also equipped with sophisticated communication abilities, particularly among the baleen species. Humpback whales are renowned for their complex songs, which can travel great distances underwater. These vocalizations are thought to play a role in mating and social interactions, showcasing the importance of sound in the vast and often murky oceanic environment. Toothed whales, like dolphins and sperm whales, utilize echolocation to navigate and hunt. By emitting clicks and listening for the returning echoes, they can detect prey and obstacles with remarkable precision, an adaptation that is especially valuable in the dark depths of the ocean.

Sharks, the apex predators of the sea, belong to a group known as elasmobranchs, which also includes rays and skates. Unlike whales, sharks are fish, and their adaptations reflect their role as highly efficient hunters. The most iconic of these adaptations is their keen sense of smell, which enables them to detect minute traces of blood in the water from miles away. This acute olfactory ability is complemented by their highly sensitive lateral line system, allowing them to detect vibrations and movements in the water, crucial for locating prey.

The body shape of sharks varies widely among species, each adapted to their specific ecological niche. The streamlined, torpedo-shaped bodies of species like the great white shark are built for speed and power, enabling them to ambush prey with explosive bursts of energy. Other species, like the hammerhead shark, have a uniquely shaped head that enhances their ability to detect prey buried in the sand through specialized electroreceptors known as ampullae of Lorenzini. These receptors allow sharks to sense the electrical fields produced by living organisms, providing a distinct advantage in hunting.

Sharks possess a unique skeletal structure composed of cartilage, rather than bone, which makes them lighter and more flexible. This adaptation, along with their buoyant liver filled with oil, helps them maintain buoyancy and maneuverability in the water. The teeth of sharks are another remarkable adaptation, with some species having multiple rows that can be replaced throughout their lifetime. This continuous supply of sharp teeth ensures they are always equipped to capture and consume prey.

Both whales and sharks face significant challenges in the modern world, largely due to human activities. Overfishing, habitat destruction, and climate change threaten their populations and the delicate balance of marine ecosystems. Whales are particularly vulnerable to ship strikes, entanglement in fishing gear, and noise pollution, which can disrupt their communication and navigation. Sharks, often targeted for their fins, are subject to overfishing and bycatch, leading to declines in many species.

Conservation efforts are critical to protect these ocean giants and the ecosystems they inhabit. Marine protected areas, sustainable fishing practices, and international agreements on species protection are essential components of conservation strategies. Public awareness and education also play a key role in fostering appreciation and understanding of these magnificent creatures, promoting actions that support their preservation.

The adaptations of whales and sharks are a testament to the incredible diversity and ingenuity of life in the ocean. These creatures, with their unique physiological and behavioral traits, demonstrate the power of evolution to shape life in diverse and challenging environments. By understanding and appreciating the adaptations of whales and sharks, we gain valuable insights into the complexities of marine ecosystems and the importance of preserving these vital habitats.

Freshwater vs. Saltwater Diverse Habitats and Their Challenges

The planet's waters are divided into two major types of aquatic environments: freshwater and saltwater, each presenting a unique set of conditions, challenges, and opportunities for the myriad of life forms they support. These habitats, though connected by the global water cycle, offer starkly contrasting worlds, each with its own dynamic ecosystems and species specially adapted to thrive within them.

Freshwater habitats, which include rivers, lakes, ponds, and wetlands, comprise only a small fraction of the Earth's water supply—about 2.5%. Despite their limited volume, these habitats are vital for the survival of countless species and for human needs. The variability in these environments is immense, with conditions ranging from the fast-flowing, oxygen-rich waters of mountain streams to the still, nutrient-laden waters of lowland lakes. Each of these settings offers distinct challenges and requires specific adaptations from its inhabitants.

The organisms living in freshwater environments must cope with a range of conditions, one of the most significant being the lower salt concentration compared to saltwater habitats. Freshwater fish, for example, have developed efficient osmoregulatory systems to prevent their bodies from absorbing excess water and losing necessary salts. This adaptation allows them to maintain homeostasis in an environment where the osmotic gradient favors water influx. Amphibians, too, have evolved permeable skin that facilitates gas exchange while minimizing water loss, allowing them to thrive in both aquatic and terrestrial settings.

In contrast, saltwater habitats cover over 70% of the Earth's surface and include oceans, seas, and estuaries. The high salinity of these environments presents a different set of challenges for marine organisms. Marine fish and other saltwater species have adapted to excrete excess salts through specialized cells in their gills, while their kidneys conserve water, enabling them to maintain internal balance in the hypertonic marine environment. The vastness and depth of the oceans further influence the life forms they host, with adaptations varying significantly from the sunlit surface waters to the dark abyssal zones.

The diversity of life in saltwater habitats is extraordinary, with coral reefs, kelp forests, and open ocean ecosystems supporting a wide array of species. Coral reefs, often compared to underwater cities, are bustling with life, offering food and shelter to numerous marine organisms. The structural complexity of these reefs provides niches for countless species, from tiny shrimp to large predatory fish, creating a highly interconnected ecosystem. Kelp forests, found in cooler waters, serve as vital habitats for fish, invertebrates, and marine mammals, with towering kelp providing both food and shelter.

While freshwater and saltwater habitats are distinct in many ways, they are interconnected through estuaries—transitional zones where rivers meet the sea. Estuaries are dynamic environments characterized by fluctuating salinity levels, tides, and nutrient inputs, making them some of the most productive ecosystems on Earth. These areas serve as nurseries for many marine species, providing a safe haven for juvenile fish and invertebrates to grow before venturing into the open ocean. The rich nutrient supply in estuaries supports diverse food webs, making them vital areas for both wildlife and human economies.

Both freshwater and saltwater habitats face significant challenges, largely due to human activities. Pollution, habitat destruction, overfishing, and climate change have profound impacts on aquatic ecosystems. Freshwater habitats are particularly vulnerable to pollution from agricultural runoff, industrial waste, and urban development, which can lead to eutrophication, harmful algal blooms, and loss of biodiversity. Dams and water diversions further alter the natural flow of rivers, affecting the migration and breeding of aquatic species.

Saltwater habitats, too, are threatened by pollution, overfishing, and climate change. Oil spills, plastic waste, and chemical pollutants contaminate marine environments, posing threats to wildlife and human health. Overfishing depletes fish stocks and disrupts marine food webs, while climate change leads to ocean warming, acidification, and sea-level rise, all of which have devastating effects on marine ecosystems. Coral reefs, in particular, are highly sensitive to these changes, with rising temperatures causing widespread coral bleaching and degradation.

Conservation efforts are crucial to protect and restore both freshwater and saltwater habitats. Initiatives to reduce pollution, establish protected areas, and promote sustainable resource management are essential for the preservation of aquatic biodiversity. Restoration projects that focus on habitat rehabilitation, such as wetland restoration and coral reef rebuilding, can help reverse some of the damage caused by human activities. Additionally, efforts to combat climate change through reducing greenhouse gas emissions and promoting renewable energy are vital for the long-term health of aquatic ecosystems.

Public awareness and education are also key components of conservation strategies. By fostering a deeper understanding of the importance of freshwater and saltwater habitats, and the threats they face, we can inspire action and promote sustainable practices. Community involvement in conservation projects, such as river cleanups and citizen science initiatives, empowers individuals to take an active role in protecting their local environments.

The diversity and complexity of freshwater and saltwater habitats are a testament to the adaptability and resilience of life on Earth. These ecosystems not only provide essential resources and services but also contribute to the cultural and economic well-being of human societies. By recognizing the value of these habitats and working towards their conservation, we can ensure that they continue to support the rich tapestry of life that depends on them.

Chapter 5

Extreme Environments Survival Against the Odds

Arctic Adaptations The Cold Warriors

In the harsh, frigid expanse of the Arctic, where temperatures can plummet to unimaginable lows and the sun disappears for months on end, life persists against all odds. This frozen wilderness, blanketed in ice and snow, is home to an array of creatures that have mastered the art of survival in one of the most unforgiving environments on Earth. These cold warriors, from polar bears to Arctic foxes, have evolved a remarkable set of adaptations that equip them to thrive amidst the ice and snow.

At the pinnacle of the Arctic food chain stands the polar bear, an iconic symbol of the region's wildlife. These majestic predators are superbly adapted to their environment, with a thick layer of blubber providing insulation against the biting cold. Their fur, which appears white but is actually translucent, serves not only as camouflage in the snowy landscape but also as an additional layer of warmth. Underneath, their skin is black, absorbing heat from the sun—a crucial adaptation during the limited daylight of Arctic summers.

Polar bears are adept swimmers, traversing vast distances in search of their primary prey, seals. Their large, paddle-like paws are perfectly suited for swimming, while the rough pads and sharp claws provide traction on ice. Seals, the mainstay of the polar bear diet, are caught through a combination of stealth and patience as bears wait by breathing holes in the ice. These hunting techniques are vital for survival in an environment where food is scarce and energy conservation is paramount.

The Arctic fox, another resident of this icy realm, is a master of adaptation. Its fur changes color with the seasons—white in winter to blend with the snow, and brown or gray in summer to match the tundra. This seasonal camouflage is not only a defense against predators but also aids in hunting small mammals and birds. The Arctic fox's compact body, short legs, and bushy tail minimize heat loss, while its thick fur provides insulation. Even its paws are covered in fur, allowing it to walk on ice and snow with ease.

The musk ox, a herbivore of the Arctic tundra, showcases another set of adaptations for survival in the cold. Stocky and robust, musk oxen are equipped with long, shaggy coats that reach almost to the ground, providing insulation and protection from the wind. Underneath, a dense layer of fine wool, known as qiviut, traps body heat. These animals travel in herds and form protective circles around their young when threatened by predators, highlighting the importance of social behavior in survival.

Birds too have mastered Arctic life, with species such as the snowy owl and the Arctic tern demonstrating remarkable resilience. The snowy owl, with its keen eyesight and silent flight, hunts lemmings and other small mammals even in the depths of the Arctic winter. Its feathers provide excellent insulation, while its ability to fly long distances in search of food ensures its survival in lean times. The Arctic tern, renowned for its long migratory journey between polar regions, takes advantage of the endless summer daylight to feed and raise its young before returning to the Antarctic.

Marine life in the Arctic also showcases extraordinary adaptations. The narwhal, known for its long, spiraled tusk, is a deep-diving cetacean that navigates the icy waters with precision. Its ability to echolocate allows it to find breathing holes in the ice, while its blubber provides insulation. The walrus, with its distinctive tusks and whiskered face, uses its formidable physique to haul out onto ice floes and access clams and mollusks on the ocean floor. Their social nature and vocal communication play significant roles in their survival.

Despite these impressive adaptations, Arctic wildlife faces unprecedented challenges due to climate change. The rapid warming of the region is causing sea ice to melt at alarming rates, threatening the habitats and hunting grounds of many species. Polar bears, in particular, are at risk as their reliance on sea ice for hunting seals becomes increasingly untenable. The loss of ice affects not only their ability to find food but also their breeding and denning practices.

The warming climate also impacts the availability of prey for Arctic foxes and other predators, leading to increased competition for food. Migratory patterns of birds may be altered, affecting breeding success and survival rates. Marine species, such as walruses and narwhals, face challenges as their icy habitats shrink and food sources become less predictable.

Conservation efforts are essential to mitigate the impacts of climate change on Arctic wildlife. International cooperation and agreements, such as the Arctic Council, play a pivotal role in addressing the environmental challenges facing the region. Protecting critical habitats, regulating shipping and industrial activities, and reducing greenhouse gas emissions are vital strategies for preserving the Arctic's unique ecosystems.

Research and monitoring are also crucial for understanding the effects of climate change and developing effective conservation strategies. Scientists study the behavior, genetics, and population dynamics of Arctic species to assess their resilience and adaptability to changing conditions. This knowledge informs policy decisions and conservation actions aimed at safeguarding the future of these cold warriors.

Public awareness and education are equally important in the effort to protect the Arctic. By highlighting the beauty and fragility of this region and its inhabitants, we can inspire action and foster a sense of responsibility for its preservation. Engaging communities, particularly Indigenous peoples whose traditional knowledge is invaluable, contributes to a more comprehensive understanding and stewardship of Arctic ecosystems.

Desert Dwellers Beating the Heat

Amidst the blistering sun and endless sands, deserts present one of the most challenging environments on Earth. Despite these harsh conditions, an astonishing array of life has adapted to call these barren landscapes home. From the resilient cacti to the elusive sand cat, desert dwellers have evolved a myriad of strategies to beat the heat and thrive in arid conditions where water is as precious as gold.

The Sahara, the Gobi, the Sonoran—each desert, though unique in its geography and climate, presents a common set of challenges: extreme temperatures, limited water, and scarce vegetation. Yet, life persists. Consider the camel, often dubbed the "ship of the desert." This iconic mammal is emblematic of desert survival. With its humps storing fat reserves, camels can endure long periods without food. Their ability to drink immense quantities of water in a single sitting, coupled with specialized kidneys that minimize water loss, makes them extraordinarily well-suited to the desert's demands.

Another master of desert survival is the fennec fox, whose large ears are not just for acute hearing but also serve as radiators to dissipate heat. Its nocturnal lifestyle helps avoid the scorching daytime temperatures, while its sandy-colored coat provides camouflage against predators. The fennec fox's ability to extract moisture from its food further exemplifies the innovative adaptations of desert creatures.

Plants, too, have devised remarkable means to thrive in deserts. Cacti, with their fleshy tissues, store water for drought periods. Their spines, a modified leaf, serve dual purposes: minimizing water loss and deterring herbivores. Some species, like the saguaro, can expand to hold more water after a rainfall, showcasing the adaptability of desert flora. Meanwhile, the mesquite tree extends its roots deep into the earth, tapping into underground water sources, a testament to nature's ingenuity in water conservation.

Desert invertebrates, often overlooked, play crucial roles in these ecosystems. The Namib Desert beetle, for instance, harvests moisture from fog. By tilting its body, the beetle allows water droplets to collect on its back and roll down to its mouth. This ingenious method of water collection is a fascinating adaptation to an environment where rain is a rarity. Similarly, the Saharan silver ant, covered in reflective hairs, withstands the midday sun by reflecting solar radiation, allowing it to forage during the hottest part of the day when predators are less active.

Reptiles, with their cold-blooded physiology, are particularly well-suited to desert life. The thorny devil, native to the Australian Outback, has a unique ability to channel water across its body surface directly to its mouth through capillary action. This adaptation, combined with its diet of ants, enables it to survive in one of the driest regions on Earth. Meanwhile, the sidewinder snake, with its distinctive sideways movement, minimizes contact with the hot desert sand, reducing body heat absorption—a clever tactic for thermoregulation.

Birds, too, have found ways to adapt to the desert's extreme conditions. The sandgrouse, for example, has feathers that can absorb and hold water, allowing it to transport moisture from distant water sources back to its young. This adaptation is vital in an environment where water is scarce and scattered. The roadrunner, an icon of the American Southwest, is another avian marvel, capable of conserving energy by reducing its activity during the hottest parts of the day. cultures have also adapted to desert life, with Indigenous peoples developing deep knowledge and techniques for living sustainably in arid landscapes. The Bedouins of the Arabian deserts, for instance, have traditionally led nomadic lifestyles, moving with their livestock to follow seasonal rains and grazing lands. Their tents, made of goat hair, provide shelter and ventilation, offering a respite from the heat. Similarly, the San people of the Kalahari have honed their skills in tracking and foraging, utilizing an intimate understanding of their environment to find water and food.

Despite these remarkable adaptations, desert ecosystems face significant threats from climate change and human activities. Overgrazing, mining, and urban expansion encroach upon these fragile habitats, disrupting the delicate balance that sustains life. Climate change exacerbates these challenges by altering precipitation patterns and increasing temperatures, further stressing already scarce water resources.

Conservation efforts are crucial to protect desert environments and the unique species that inhabit them. Establishing protected areas, promoting sustainable land-use practices, and restoring degraded landscapes are key strategies in preserving desert biodiversity. Research and monitoring, particularly in understanding the impacts of climate change, are vital for informed conservation actions.

Education and community engagement are equally important in desert conservation. By raising awareness of the value and vulnerability of desert ecosystems, we can inspire actions that support their preservation. Local communities, with their traditional knowledge and stewardship, play a pivotal role in conservation efforts. Collaborations between governments, NGOs, and Indigenous peoples can foster sustainable practices that benefit both people and the environment.

Rainforest Resilience Surviving in a Green World

The rainforest, a verdant tapestry of life, teems with an astonishing diversity of species. Beneath its dense canopy, a complex web of interactions unfolds, showcasing an ecosystem both resilient and fragile. The rainforest's unique environment, characterized by high rainfall and humidity, creates conditions ripe for life to flourish, but also presents challenges that demand remarkable adaptations.

Consider the towering trees that dominate the rainforest skyline. These giants, such as the kapok and the Brazil nut tree, form the backbone of the rainforest structure. They have evolved to grow rapidly, racing towards the sunlight in a crowded environment where light is a precious commodity. Their buttress roots, sprawling outwards like the skeletal fingers of a giant, provide stability in the shallow, nutrient-poor soil. These roots not only anchor the trees but also serve as conduits for nutrient exchange with other plant species through complex mycorrhizal networks.

Among the branches and leaves, a myriad of creatures have carved out niches. The canopy is alive with sound and movement. Monkeys, such as howlers and spider monkeys, swing effortlessly from branch to branch, their prehensile tails acting as a fifth limb. This arboreal lifestyle allows them to access food sources like fruits and leaves while avoiding ground-dwelling predators. Birds, too, are prominent residents of the canopy. The resplendent quetzal and the harpy eagle each exhibit adaptations that enable them to thrive in this lush environment. The quetzal's brilliant plumage provides camouflage among the vibrant foliage, while the powerful talons of the harpy eagle make it a formidable predator.

On the forest floor, where sunlight barely penetrates, a different set of challenges awaits. Plants have adapted to low-light conditions by developing large, broad leaves to capture as much sunlight as possible. Ferns and understory shrubs thrive here, their growth often reliant on symbiotic relationships with fungi, which help them extract nutrients from the poor soil. The leaf litter is teeming with activity, a world unto itself where ants, beetles, and other decomposers break down organic matter, recycling nutrients back into the ecosystem.

The rainforest's biodiversity is not limited to its flora and fauna. Insects, particularly ants, play critical roles in maintaining the balance of this ecosystem. Leafcutter ants, for instance, are diligent farmers, cutting leaves to cultivate fungus in their underground nests. This mutualistic relationship benefits both the ants and the rainforest, as the decomposition process enriches the soil. Similarly, pollinators such as bees and butterflies are essential for the reproduction of many plant species, ensuring the continuation of the rainforest's intricate life cycle.

Amphibians, like the poison dart frog, are another testament to the rainforest's adaptability. These frogs display vibrant colors as a warning to predators about their toxicity—a defense mechanism honed over millennia. Their permeable skin allows for efficient gas exchange in the humid environment, though it also makes them vulnerable to environmental changes, highlighting the delicate balance they maintain with their surroundings.

The rainforest's resilience is remarkable, yet it is not invincible. Human activities, such as deforestation for agriculture and logging, have significant impacts on these vital ecosystems. The loss of trees not only reduces biodiversity but also disrupts the carbon and water cycles, contributing to climate change and altering rainfall patterns. As trees are removed, the soil becomes more susceptible to erosion, further degrading the habitat.

Conservation efforts are crucial to protect the rainforest and its inhabitants. Establishing protected areas and promoting sustainable land-use practices are essential strategies to preserve these ecosystems. Reforestation projects, which involve planting native tree species, can help restore degraded areas and provide corridors for wildlife movement. Additionally, supporting Indigenous communities in managing their lands is vital, as they possess invaluable traditional knowledge and practices that contribute to rainforest conservation.

Research plays a key role in understanding the complexities of rainforest ecosystems and the impacts of human activities. Scientists study the interactions between species, monitor changes in biodiversity, and assess the effects of climate change on rainforest dynamics. This information is essential for developing effective conservation policies and strategies.

Public awareness and education are equally important components of rainforest conservation. By raising awareness about the vital role rainforests play in global biodiversity, climate regulation, and human well-being, we can inspire action and foster a sense of stewardship. Collaborations between governments, NGOs, and local communities are crucial in implementing conservation initiatives and promoting sustainable development.

High Altitude Adaptations Life on the Edge

Perched on the precipice of survival, life finds a way to flourish in the dizzying heights of the world's mountain ranges. These high-altitude environments, characterized by thin air, extreme temperatures, and rugged terrain, present formidable challenges to the organisms that inhabit them. Yet, through a series of remarkable adaptations, a diverse array of species has made these seemingly inhospitable regions their home, demonstrating nature's incredible resilience.

Consider the snow leopard, a phantom of the mountains, whose solitary existence unfolds amidst the jagged peaks and windswept ridges of Central

Asia. This elusive big cat is a master of its domain, equipped with a thick, smoky-gray coat that provides insulation against the biting cold. Its large, powerful paws act as natural snowshoes, allowing it to traverse the deep snow with ease. The long, muscular tail serves a dual purpose: maintaining balance on precarious ledges and providing warmth when wrapped around the body during rest. These adaptations are essential for stalking prey such as ibex and blue sheep in the challenging alpine terrain.

Birds, too, have carved out niches in these lofty realms. The bar-headed goose, renowned for its high-altitude migrations over the Himalayas, possesses a suite of physiological traits that enable it to thrive in low-oxygen environments. Its ability to increase oxygen uptake through efficient breathing and enhanced blood circulation is complemented by a unique hemoglobin structure that binds oxygen more effectively. This allows the goose to maintain energy levels during long flights at altitudes where the air is thin, a testament to nature's ingenuity.

Among the rugged cliffs and rocky outcrops, the Himalayan tahr exemplifies the balance between agility and strength. These nimble ungulates have evolved specialized hooves with a rough, textured surface that provides grip on steep, slippery slopes. Their muscular build and keen sense of balance allow them to navigate the treacherous terrain with confidence, evading predators and accessing scarce vegetation. The tahr's dense, woolly coat offers protection against the cold, while its social structure, forming small herds, enhances survival through communal vigilance.

The plant life in high-altitude regions is equally remarkable, displaying adaptations that defy the harsh conditions. The edelweiss, a symbol of alpine endurance, has developed a unique strategy to combat intense ultraviolet radiation. Its star-shaped leaves are covered in tiny white hairs that reflect sunlight, reducing water loss and protecting the plant from the sun's damaging rays. This adaptation, coupled with a deep root system that anchors it in shallow soil, allows the edelweiss to thrive in rocky crevices where few other plants can survive.

In the Andes, the vicuña—a wild relative of the domesticated alpaca—has honed its adaptations to the cold, windy altiplano. Its fine, silky fleece provides exceptional insulation, while its large lungs and efficient metabolism enable it to extract oxygen from the thin air. The vicuña's social behavior, forming tight-knit groups, enhances protection against predators and harsh weather, demonstrating the importance of cooperation in survival.

Insects, often overlooked, play crucial roles in high-altitude ecosystems. The Himalayan jumping spider, for example, is one of the highest-dwelling non-flying arthropods. It survives by feeding on small insects and utilizing its excellent vision to hunt in the sparse vegetation. Its ability to withstand extreme temperatures and low oxygen levels highlights the diversity of strategies employed by life at altitude.

Despite these remarkable adaptations, high-altitude ecosystems face growing challenges from climate change and human activities. The warming climate threatens to alter the delicate balance of these environments, as rising temperatures and shifting precipitation patterns impact both plant and animal life. Glacial melt, a critical source of freshwater for many high-altitude regions, poses significant risks to downstream communities and ecosystems.

Conservation efforts are vital to protect these unique landscapes and their inhabitants. Establishing protected areas, promoting sustainable tourism, and supporting local communities in conservation initiatives are essential strategies for preserving high-altitude biodiversity. Research plays a crucial role in understanding the impacts of climate change and human activities, informing policy decisions and conservation actions.

Education and public awareness are equally important in fostering a sense of stewardship for high-altitude environments. By highlighting the beauty and vulnerability of these regions and their inhabitants, we can inspire action and encourage sustainable practices. Collaboration between governments, NGOs, and Indigenous communities is key to implementing effective conservation strategies that benefit both people and the environment.

Deep Sea Adaptations The Last Frontier

Beneath the tranquil surface of the oceans lies a world of mystery and wonder, the deep sea—a realm so remote and alien that it might as well be another planet. This vast, dark expanse, with pressures so immense they could crush a human, presents a host of challenges to the creatures that inhabit it. Yet, life flourishes here, revealing a staggering array of adaptations that allow these organisms to survive in one of Earth's most extreme environments.

The deep sea begins where sunlight can no longer penetrate, plunging the world into perpetual darkness. In this abyssal zone, many organisms have evolved bioluminescence, the ability to produce light through chemical reactions within their bodies. This adaptation serves multiple purposes: communication, mating, camouflage, and hunting. The anglerfish, for example, uses a glowing lure that dangles from its head to attract prey in the pitch-black waters. This eerie light, a beacon in the depths, is both a tool of survival and a symbol of the ingenuity of life.

Pressure in the deep sea can exceed 1,000 times that at the surface, a challenge that deep-sea creatures meet with specialized adaptations. The gelatinous bodies of many deep-sea fish help them withstand these crushing forces without the need for bulky structures. The absence of a swim bladder, which can be easily compressed, is another common trait among these fish, allowing them to maintain buoyancy without the risk of implosion. Instead, they rely on other methods, such as oil-rich livers, to achieve buoyancy.

Food is scarce in the deep sea, and many creatures have adapted to this scarcity with unique feeding strategies. The gulper eel, with its enormous mouth and expandable stomach, can consume prey much larger than itself, ensuring it capitalizes on opportunities when they arise. Scavengers like the hagfish feed on the carcasses of marine animals that drift down from the surface, playing a crucial role in nutrient recycling in this nutrient-poor environment. These opportunistic feeding habits are essential for survival in a world where meals are few and far between.

In the deepest trenches, life persists in ways that continue to astonish scientists. Hydrothermal vent communities, discovered only in the late 20th century, showcase ecosystems that thrive without sunlight, relying instead on chemosynthesis. Here, bacteria convert the toxic chemicals emitted by the vents into energy, forming the base of a unique food web. Giant tube worms, clams, and shrimp form symbiotic relationships with these bacteria, deriving sustenance from the chemical-rich waters. This remarkable adaptation highlights the diversity of life and its ability to exploit even the most inhospitable environments.

The deep sea is also home to some of the most enigmatic creatures on Earth. The vampire squid, with its crimson skin and webbed arms, uses bioluminescent displays to confuse predators. Its ability to survive on minimal oxygen is a testament to its efficiency in conserving energy. The elusive giant squid, once thought to be a myth, roams the depths, its massive eyes adapted to detect the faintest glimmers of light in the darkness.

Despite its isolation, the deep sea is not immune to human impact. Deep-sea mining, pollution, and climate change pose significant threats to these fragile ecosystems. The slow growth rates and long lifespans of many deep-sea species make them particularly vulnerable to disturbances. As we venture into the last frontier, it is crucial to balance exploration with conservation.

Scientific research is vital for understanding the complexities of deep-sea ecosystems and the impacts of human activities. Advances in technology, such as remotely operated vehicles and submersibles, have allowed scientists to explore these depths and document the incredible diversity of life. This knowledge is essential for informing conservation efforts and developing policies to protect these unique habitats.

Public awareness and education play a key role in fostering a sense of stewardship for the deep sea. By sharing the wonders of this hidden world and its inhabitants, we can inspire action and promote sustainable practices. International cooperation is crucial in addressing the global challenges facing the deep sea. Collaborative efforts between governments, scientists, and conservation organizations can lead to effective strategies for preserving these ecosystems.

Chapter 6

Unique Strategies for Defense and Predation

Defensive Mechanisms Armor, Spines, and Toxins

In the grand theater of nature, survival often hinges on the ability to avoid becoming someone else's meal. Through millennia of evolution, a dazzling array of defensive mechanisms has developed to protect organisms from predators. From the impenetrable armor of turtles to the lethal toxins of the poison dart frog, these adaptations are as diverse as they are fascinating, each a testament to the relentless arms race between predator and prey.

Armor, one of nature's most ancient forms of defense, offers a physical barrier against would-be attackers. Turtles and tortoises, with their iconic shells, exemplify this strategy. Their shells, composed of a fusion of rib bones and dermal plates, are a formidable refuge that can deter even the most persistent predators. This evolutionary marvel provides not only protection but also support for the turtle's internal organs. Similarly, the armadillo's bony plates serve as a shield, allowing it to curl into a compact ball, effectively safeguarding its vulnerable underbelly.

In the aquatic realm, the pangolin's marine counterpart, the sea urchin, dons a suit of spines that deters predators with both physical and sometimes toxic defenses. These spines, which can be venomous in some species, not only protect the urchin from predation but also serve as tools for locomotion and interaction with their environment. The pufferfish, another master of defense, relies on its ability to inflate its body, transforming into a spiky, unpalatable sphere when threatened. This sudden change in shape and size can startle and ward off predators, showcasing a combination of physiological and structural defense mechanisms.

Beyond physical defenses, many organisms have evolved chemical means of deterring predators. The poison dart frog, with its vibrant colors, serves as a vivid warning of its toxicity. These frogs secrete potent alkaloids through their skin, substances acquired through their diet of ants and other small invertebrates. This chemical arsenal is so effective that a single frog contains enough toxin to incapacitate multiple predators, a clear message to would-be attackers. Similarly, the monarch butterfly, though less lethal, employs a strategy of chemical defense by sequestering toxins from milkweed plants during its larval stage. This makes the adult butterfly distasteful to birds, which quickly learn to avoid these brightly colored insects.

Plants, too, have developed intricate defense strategies, often employing a combination of mechanical and chemical deterrents. The rose's iconic thorns serve as a physical barrier against herbivores, while many plants produce secondary metabolites—such as alkaloids and tannins—that deter feeding through toxicity or unpleasant taste. In some cases, plants can even release volatile organic compounds that attract predators of their herbivores, an indirect but effective means of defense.

Mimicry, both in appearance and behavior, is another fascinating defensive strategy. Some species, like the harmless milk snake, mimic the coloration of the venomous coral snake, gaining protection through deception. This form of Batesian mimicry relies on predators' learned avoidance of the model species, effectively reducing predation on the mimic. In contrast, Müllerian mimicry involves two or more unpalatable species evolving similar warning signals, reinforcing the avoidance behavior of predators. This cooperative form of mimicry benefits all participating species by spreading the cost of educating predators across multiple organisms.

In the insect world, camouflage is a key defensive strategy. The leaf insect, with its uncanny resemblance to a green leaf, can remain undetected by predators, effectively blending into its environment. This form of crypsis is widespread, with many insects, reptiles, and even birds evolving patterns and colors that help them avoid detection.

Behavioral adaptations also play a crucial role in defense. Meerkats, for instance, employ a strategy of communal vigilance, where individuals take turns standing guard against predators. This cooperative behavior increases the chances of detecting threats early, allowing the group to seek refuge. Similarly, the opossum exhibits tonic immobility, or "playing dead," a behavior that can dissuade predators that prefer live prey.

While these defensive mechanisms are remarkably effective, they are not infallible. The evolutionary arms race between predator and prey drives continuous adaptation, with predators developing counter-strategies to overcome these defenses. This dynamic interplay shapes the diversity of life and the complexity of ecosystems. activities, however, pose a significant threat to the balance of these natural interactions. Habitat destruction, climate change, and pollution can disrupt ecosystems and diminish the effectiveness of these evolutionary strategies. Conservation efforts are essential to preserve biodiversity and maintain the integrity of ecosystems where these fascinating adaptations have evolved.

Research and education play vital roles in understanding and protecting these natural defenses. By studying the mechanisms and interactions within ecosystems, scientists can gain insights into the evolutionary processes that drive biodiversity. Public awareness and appreciation of the intricate relationships in nature can inspire conservation actions and promote sustainable practices.

Predatory Tactics Stalking, Ambush, and Cooperation

In the relentless pursuit of survival, predators have evolved a remarkable suite of tactics to capture prey. These strategies, honed over millennia, showcase the ingenuity and adaptability of life in the natural world. Stalking, ambush, and cooperation are among the most effective methods employed by predators, each demonstrating a unique approach to overcoming the challenges of hunting.

Stalking is a game of patience and precision, where predators rely on stealth and timing to close in on their prey. The big cats, such as lions and leopards, are masters of this technique. With their keen senses and powerful bodies, they silently track their quarry, inching ever closer before launching a sudden and decisive attack. The leopard, in particular, exemplifies this method, using its spotted coat as camouflage to blend seamlessly into the dappled shadows of the savannah. It moves with deliberate grace, minimizing noise and remaining downwind to avoid detection. As the gap narrows, the anticipation builds, and with a burst of speed, the leopard pounces, delivering a swift and lethal blow.

In the aquatic realm, the great white shark employs a similar strategy. Its acute sense of smell and ability to detect the faint electrical signals emitted by prey allow it to stalk with precision. Sharks often circle their target, assessing its size and behavior, before accelerating with explosive speed to capture unsuspecting seals or fish. This calculated approach, combined with the shark's formidable size and strength, makes it one of the ocean's most efficient hunters.

Ambush tactics rely on surprise and the element of the unexpected. Predators employing this strategy often lie in wait, concealed within their environment, until the moment is right to strike. The crocodile, with its prehistoric lineage, epitomizes the ambush predator. It lurks beneath the water's surface, barely visible, as it waits for prey to approach the water's edge. With a sudden eruption of power, the crocodile lunges, its jaws snapping shut with incredible force. This burst of aggression, coupled with its ability to remain motionless for extended periods, makes the crocodile a formidable predator in its watery domain.

On land, the trapdoor spider employs a similar tactic. It constructs a hidden burrow with a silken lid, lying in wait just beneath the surface. As an unsuspecting insect passes by, the spider springs forth with lightning speed, capturing its prey in an instant. This ambush strategy is a marvel of engineering and timing, showcasing the spider's ability to exploit its environment to its advantage.

Cooperation in hunting reveals a fascinating dimension of predatory behavior, where individuals work together to achieve a common goal. Wolves, with their complex social structures, are adept at cooperative hunting. Packs communicate through vocalizations and body language, coordinating their movements to encircle and isolate prey. This teamwork allows wolves to tackle larger animals, such as elk and deer, that would be formidable opponents for a lone wolf. The pack's ability to strategize and adapt to the behavior of their quarry underscores the intelligence and social bonds that underpin cooperative hunting.

In the ocean, orcas, or killer whales, exhibit similarly sophisticated hunting tactics. These apex predators use a combination of vocalizations and synchronized movements to herd fish into tight balls, making them easier to capture. In some regions, orcas have been observed working together to create waves that wash seals off ice floes, demonstrating a remarkable level of problem-solving and cooperation. This collective intelligence and adaptability highlight the orca's position as one of the ocean's most formidable predators.

The success of these predatory tactics hinges on a predator's ability to adapt to its environment and the behavior of its prey. This dynamic interplay drives the evolution of both predator and prey, resulting in a continuous cycle of adaptation and counter-adaptation. As prey species evolve new defenses, such as heightened vigilance or faster escape responses, predators must refine their strategies to maintain their edge. activities, however, have introduced new challenges to this delicate balance. Habitat destruction, climate change, and overfishing can disrupt ecosystems and alter the availability of prey, forcing predators to adapt or face decline. Conservation efforts are essential to preserving the habitats and biodiversity that support these intricate relationships.

Research into predatory behavior provides valuable insights into the complexities of ecosystems and the evolutionary pressures that shape life on Earth. By understanding the strategies and adaptations of predators, scientists can better assess the health of ecosystems and identify conservation priorities.

Education and public awareness are crucial in fostering appreciation and respect for predators and their role in nature. By highlighting the beauty and intricacy of predatory tactics, we can inspire action and promote sustainable practices that protect these vital components of the natural world.

The Role of Senses in Survival Sight, Smell, and Hearing

In the intricate dance of survival, senses are the tools through which animals interpret and interact with their environment. These sensory systems are finely tuned instruments that provide the information necessary to find food, evade predators, and navigate the world. Among the most critical senses are sight, smell, and hearing—each playing a unique and vital role in the survival strategies of countless species.

Sight, perhaps the most immediately recognizable of the senses, offers a window into the world that is both vast and detailed. In the animal kingdom, vision can vary dramatically, with adaptations tailored to specific ecological niches. The eagle, with its extraordinary eyesight, can spot a rabbit from miles away, its sharp focus and acute perception enabling it to hunt effectively. This avian predator benefits from a high density of photoreceptor cells in its retinas and a large fovea, which provide exceptional visual acuity and depth perception. These adaptations allow eagles to make precise calculations of distance and speed, critical for capturing fast-moving prey.

On the other hand, the mantis shrimp possesses one of the most complex visual systems known to science. With up to 16 types of photoreceptor cells, compared to the human's three, the mantis shrimp can detect a spectrum of colors and polarized light, unseen by most other creatures. This rich visual information is crucial for communication and locating prey within the vibrant coral reefs they inhabit, illustrating the profound diversity of visual adaptations in the natural world.

Smell, an often underestimated sense, is a powerful tool for survival, particularly in environments where visibility is limited. Canines, such as wolves and domestic dogs, exemplify the importance of olfactory capabilities. With an olfactory system that contains up to 300 million scent receptors—compared to a human's five million—dogs can detect and differentiate a myriad of scents. This acute sense of smell aids in tracking prey, identifying territory, and locating mates. The ability to perceive pheromones and other chemical signals allows these animals to navigate their social and physical worlds with remarkable precision.

In the marine environment, sharks are among the most renowned for their olfactory prowess. They can detect a single drop of blood in an Olympic-sized swimming pool, a testament to their sensitivity. This acute sense of smell is essential for locating prey in the vast and often murky ocean, providing them with a critical advantage in their role as apex predators. The olfactory lobes in a shark's brain are highly developed, allowing them to process complex scent trails and hone in on potential food sources.

Hearing, the third pillar of survival senses, provides animals with auditory cues that are crucial for communication and environmental awareness. Bats, masters of echolocation, emit high-frequency sounds and listen for the echoes that bounce back from objects around them. This acoustic radar allows them to navigate and hunt with precision in complete darkness, locating insects with astounding accuracy.

The bat's ability to process these echoes rapidly and interpret them as spatial information is a remarkable adaptation that showcases the intricacies of auditory perception.

Cetaceans, like dolphins and whales, also rely heavily on sound to understand their surroundings. In the ocean, where light penetrates only to shallow depths, sound travels far and wide. Dolphins use echolocation to hunt and communicate, producing clicks and whistles that carry through the water. These sounds are reflected back from objects, providing a detailed auditory map of their environment. This ability to "see" with sound is indispensable for navigating the vast, featureless expanses of the ocean.

The interplay between these senses allows animals to create a comprehensive picture of their surroundings, enhancing their ability to respond to challenges and opportunities. However, the reliance on particular senses varies among species, shaped by evolutionary pressures and environmental contexts. For instance, nocturnal animals often have heightened senses of smell and hearing to compensate for limited vision in low-light conditions. activities pose significant challenges to these natural adaptations. Habitat destruction, pollution, and climate change can disrupt sensory environments, leading to disorientation and stress for wildlife. Noise pollution, in particular, has become a growing concern, as it interferes with communication and echolocation in marine and terrestrial species. The increase in anthropogenic noise can mask important acoustic signals, making it difficult for animals to locate food, avoid predators, and find mates.

Conservation efforts aimed at preserving sensory habitats are crucial for maintaining biodiversity. Protecting areas from excessive noise and light pollution, restoring natural landscapes, and ensuring clean air and water can help mitigate the impacts of human activity on animal senses. Research into the sensory ecology of species provides valuable insights into how they interact with their environment and respond to changes, informing conservation strategies.

Education and public awareness are key components in promoting the protection of sensory habitats. By highlighting the importance of senses in survival and the challenges posed by human activities, we can inspire collective action to safeguard these vital aspects of the natural world. Collaborative efforts between governments, scientists, and conservation organizations can lead to effective policies and practices that support the resilience of wildlife.

Mimicry and Deception Nature's Tricksters

In the grand tapestry of life, mimicry and deception stand out as some of nature's most cunning strategies. These tactics, employed by an array of species, are not just about survival but are a testament to the intricate dance of evolution. Through mimicry and deception, creatures have developed astonishing methods to avoid predators, ensnare prey, and even engage in reproductive success, each illustrating a unique facet of nature's ingenuity.

Mimicry, at its core, involves one species evolving to resemble another, gaining an advantage by association. This evolutionary strategy falls into several categories, with Batesian and Müllerian mimicry being the most prominent. Batesian mimicry is a fascinating ruse where a harmless species takes on the appearance of a harmful one. The classic example is the resemblance between the non-venomous milk snake and the venomous coral snake. Predators, wary of the coral snake's lethal bite, often avoid both species, thus granting the milk snake a reprieve from predation. This form of mimicry relies heavily on the predator's learned experiences, turning fear into a powerful ally for the mimic.

Müllerian mimicry, on the other hand, involves two or more unpalatable or harmful species evolving similar warning signals. The convergence in appearance reinforces the avoidance behavior in predators, benefiting all parties involved. Consider the case of the monarch and viceroy butterflies. For years, it was believed that the viceroy mimicked the toxic monarch to avoid predation. However, further research revealed that the viceroy is also unpalatable, making this an example of Müllerian mimicry. Here, both species share the cost and benefit of educating predators, reinforcing the "do not eat" message.

Beyond these classic forms, mimicry extends into realms more nuanced and complex. Aggressive mimicry, for instance, involves predators or parasites that resemble harmless or beneficial entities to access their prey or host. The anglerfish, lurking in the ocean's depths, uses a fleshy lure that mimics the appearance of a small fish or worm. Unsuspecting prey, drawn to this enticing bait, soon find themselves engulfed by the angler's gaping jaws. This form of deception highlights the predator's ability to manipulate perception, turning the tables on their prey.

In the insect world, the orchid mantis provides a spectacular example of aggressive mimicry. Resembling the delicate petals of an orchid, this mantis lures pollinators in search of nectar. Instead of a sweet reward, the pollinators meet their demise as the mantis strikes with lightning speed. The mantis's appearance as a benign flower is a masterstroke of evolutionary adaptation, blending beauty and peril in a seamless facade.

Deception in nature is not limited to visual mimicry. Acoustic mimicry offers another dimension to this strategy. Some birds, like the lyrebird, have mastered the art of sound imitation, replicating the calls of other species and even mechanical noises. While primarily a tool for attracting mates, this ability can also deter competitors or predators by mimicking the calls of more dominant or dangerous species.

The world of plants is not exempt from these deceptive strategies. Some plants, known as myrmecophytes, have evolved to form symbiotic relationships with ants by mimicking ant pheromones. These plants provide shelter and nectar, while the ants offer protection against herbivores. The plants' ability to mimic chemical signals ensures the ants' loyalty, creating a mutualistic bond that benefits both parties.

Mimicry and deception also play crucial roles in reproductive strategies. Some male insects, like certain fireflies, mimic the mating signals of females from other species. When the duped males approach, they become prey instead of partners. This deadly deception serves as a reminder of the fine line between attraction and danger in the natural world.

In the realm of cephalopods, the octopus stands as a master of disguise. With the ability to change color, texture, and even shape, the octopus can blend into its surroundings or mimic other sea creatures. The mimic octopus takes this to an extreme, imitating the appearance and behavior of venomous animals like lionfish and sea snakes to deter predators. This versatility in mimicry showcases the octopus's remarkable adaptability and intelligence. activities, however, threaten the delicate balance that supports these evolutionary strategies. Habitat destruction, pollution, and climate change disrupt ecosystems, potentially leading to the loss of both mimic and model species. Conservation efforts are vital to preserving the environments that allow these intricate relationships to flourish.

Understanding mimicry and deception provides valuable insights into the evolutionary pressures and ecological interactions that shape biodiversity. Research into these strategies reveals the complex webs of influence and adaptation that connect species within ecosystems. By studying these interactions, scientists can better assess the health of ecosystems and develop effective conservation strategies.

Public awareness and education play essential roles in promoting the protection of natural habitats. By highlighting the wonders of mimicry and deception, we can inspire appreciation and action to preserve these fascinating aspects of the natural world. Collaborative efforts between governments, scientists, and conservation organizations are crucial for developing policies that support biodiversity and ecosystem resilience.

The Balance of Power Predator-Prey Dynamics

In the intricate web of life, predator-prey dynamics form the cornerstone of ecological balance. This relationship is a delicate dance of survival, where the fates of both hunters and the hunted are intertwined in a perpetual cycle of adaptation and counter-adaptation. Understanding these dynamics reveals the complexity and elegance of nature's design, where each player has evolved strategies to outwit, outlast, and outmaneuver the other.

Predators, the relentless pursuers of prey, have evolved a myriad of adaptations to enhance their hunting prowess. Speed, stealth, strength, and sensory acuity are just a few of the traits that have been honed through natural selection. The cheetah, for instance, is a marvel of evolutionary engineering, capable of reaching speeds up to 70 miles per hour in short bursts. This incredible velocity, combined with a flexible spine and powerful muscles, makes the cheetah an apex hunter on the African plains. Yet, even with such advantages, the cheetah's success rate is only about 50%, highlighting the challenges predators face in securing their next meal.

In contrast, prey species have developed their own arsenal of defenses to evade capture. Speed and agility are common traits among many animals, allowing them to escape the clutches of predators. Consider the Thompson's gazelle, whose zigzagging sprint can outmaneuver the linear chase of a cheetah. Other prey species rely on camouflage and mimicry to blend into their surroundings or deceive their predators. The peppered moth, with its speckled wings, can seamlessly vanish against the bark of trees, evading the watchful eyes of birds.

Beyond physical adaptations, behavioral strategies play a critical role in predator-prey interactions. Many prey species have developed sophisticated alarm systems to warn of impending danger. Prairie dogs, for example, use a series of vocalizations to communicate the presence and type of predator, enabling the colony to seek shelter in their burrows. This communal vigilance increases the survival chances of the group, demonstrating the power of cooperation and communication in the wild.

Predator-prey dynamics are not merely a series of individual encounters but are integral to the health and stability of ecosystems. Predators help regulate prey populations, preventing overgrazing and maintaining biodiversity. In turn, the availability of prey influences predator numbers, creating a feedback loop that helps stabilize population sizes over time. This balance can be disrupted by external factors, such as human interference, leading to cascading effects throughout the ecosystem.

The introduction or removal of predators can have profound impacts on prey populations and the wider environment. The reintroduction of wolves to Yellowstone National Park in the 1990s serves as a compelling example. Wolves had been extirpated from the park for decades, leading to an overabundance of elk, which in turn overgrazed vegetation and altered the landscape. With the return of wolves, elk numbers were brought under control, allowing vegetation to recover and promoting a resurgence of biodiversity. This trophic cascade illustrates the critical role predators play in shaping ecosystems and maintaining ecological balance. activities, however, continue to pose significant threats to predator-prey dynamics. Habitat destruction, pollution, and climate change can disrupt these relationships, leading to imbalances that threaten biodiversity. Overhunting and poaching of predator species can lead to unchecked prey populations, resulting in habitat degradation and loss of plant and animal diversity. Conversely, the decline of prey species due to habitat loss and fragmentation can lead to reduced predator numbers and even extinction.

Conservation efforts are essential to preserving the delicate equilibrium of predator-prey dynamics. Protecting habitats, establishing wildlife corridors, and implementing sustainable hunting practices can help maintain the natural balance. Rewilding initiatives, which involve the reintroduction of native species, can restore ecological functions and enhance biodiversity.

Research into predator-prey interactions provides valuable insights into ecosystem health and resilience. By studying these relationships, scientists can better understand the complex webs of influence and adaptation that connect species within ecosystems. This knowledge is crucial for developing effective conservation strategies and mitigating the impacts of human activities on natural habitats.

Education and public awareness play vital roles in promoting the protection of ecosystems and the species that inhabit them. By highlighting the importance of predator-prey dynamics, we can inspire appreciation and action to preserve these fundamental aspects of the natural world. Collaborative efforts between governments, scientists, and conservation organizations are necessary to develop policies that support biodiversity and ecosystem resilience.